Edgar Cayce on
Soul Symbolism

Selected Titles by Kevin J. Todeschi

The Best Dream Book Ever

Contemporary Cayce (with Henry Reed)

Dream Images and Symbols

Edgar Cayce on Auras and Colors (with Carol Ann Liaros)

Edgar Cayce on Mastering Your Spiritual Growth

Edgar Cayce on Reincarnation and Family Karma

Edgar Cayce on Soul Mates

Edgar Cayce on the Akashic Records

Edgar Cayce on Vibrations

Edgar Cayce's Twelve Lessons in Personal Spirituality

Edgar Cayce on Soul Symbolism

Creating Life Seals, Aura Charts, and Understanding the Revelation

By Kevin J. Todeschi

Yazdan Publishing • Virginia Beach • Virginia

Published by:
Yazdan Publishing
P.O. Box 4604
Virginia Beach, VA 23454

ISBN-13: 978-0-9845672-9-4

Cover art: The Edgar Cayce Aura Chart, oil on canvas,
70" x 50", 1967-1969, by Ingo Swann

Text and design layout by Cathy Merchand

*To that spark of Divinity within humankind
that impels each of us on a search toward who
we really are and what we should be about*

On Self-Knowledge

And a man said, "Speak to us of Self-Knowledge."
And he answered, saying:
Your hearts know in silence the secrets of the days
*   and the nights.*
But your ears thirst for the sound of your heart's knowledge.
You would know in words that which you have always
*   known in thought.*
You would touch with your fingers the naked body
*   of your dreams.*

And it is well you should.
The hidden well-spring of your soul must needs rise and run
*   murmuring to the sea;*
And the treasure of your infinite depths would be revealed
*   to your eyes.*
But let there be no scales to weigh your unknown treasure;
And seek not the depths of your knowledge with staff
*   or sounding line.*
For self is a sea boundless and measureless.

Say not, "I have found the truth," but rather, "I have
*   found a truth."*
Say not, "I have found the path of the soul." Say rather, "I
*   have met the soul walking upon my path."*
For the soul walks upon all paths.
The soul walks not upon a line, neither does it grow
*   like a reed.*
The soul unfolds itself, like a lotus of countless petals.

Kahlil Gibran, The Prophet

Contents

Introduction .... *ix*

Part 1: *Life Seals*

Chapter 1: The Life Seal as a Tool for Self-Awareness 1
Chapter 2: Exploring the Symbolism of Life Seals 17
Chapter 3: Creating Your Own Life Seal 29

Part 2: *Aura Charts*

Chapter 4: The Aura Chart as a Map of the Soul's Journey 51
Chapter 5: Exploring the Symbolism of Aura Charts 71
Chapter 6: Creating Your Own Aura Chart 91

Part 3: *The Revelation*

Chapter 7: The Revelation as a Symbolic Journey in
Personal Consciousness 113
Chapter 8: Archetypal Imagery and Revelation Symbolism 153
Chapter 9: Meditation, the Physical Body, and the Lord's Prayer ... 165

Conclusion *173*

Appendices

*Appendix A: Edgar Cayce's Symbolism for Life Seals and Aura
Charts* *179*
Appendix B: Edgar Cayce's Symbolism for the Revelation *221*
Appendix C: References and Recommended Reading *235*

Introduction

The phrase "know thyself" was immortalized by the Greeks at Delphi's Temple of Apollo. Written as an inscription ("Gnothi Seauton") over the entrance to the temple, visitors from throughout the known world came to Delphi seeking the wisdom of the god Apollo through his human representative and prophetess, the Oracle at Delphi. Perhaps the inscription served as a reminder to those seeking the advice of the gods that knowledge of the outside world and even prophecy were subservient to self-knowledge, personal awareness, and an understanding of one's true self.

According to Plato's dialogue "Phaedrus," this same sentiment was echoed by the Greek philosopher Socrates who reportedly stated, "I can't as yet 'know myself,' as the inscription at Delphi enjoins, and so long as that ignorance remains it seems to me ridiculous to inquire into extraneous matters." (Hamilton, *Plato,* pg. 478)

This search to know one's self is often mirrored in ancient stories, fables, and fairy tales that seek insights to the very-human question, "Who am I?" through a variety of myths, themes, and symbols. The desire to investigate the nature of the self has also been at the heart of scientific and psychological efforts since the beginning of the twentieth century, which have attempted to understand and explore the nature of the unconscious mind. In this regard Sigmund Freud (1856-1939), Austrian physician, neurologist, and founder of psychoanalysis, holds an important position. His theories regarding dreams as well as his work attempting to understand the psychological basis of neurotic illnesses laid the groundwork for those whose later work would continue to explore the unconscious.

Carl Jung (1875-1961), a student of Freud's and the founder of the analytical school of psychology, called Sigmund Freud, "the pioneer who first tried to explore empirically the unconscious background of consciousness." (Jung, *Man and His Symbols,* pg. 8) In addition to a wealth of information on dreams, Jung's own work stressed the importance of self-realization or individuation–the process in which each individual is brought into a harmonious and balanced relationship with every aspect of his or her true self. He came to realize that the language of the brain was symbols and found it hard to understand why that portion of the mind that produced symbols remained virtually unexplored: "It seems almost incredible that though we receive signals from it every night, deciphering these communications seems too tedious for any but a few people to be bothered with . . . " (Jung, *Man and His Symbols,* pg. 93)

A contemporary of Freud and Jung, Hermann Rorschach (1884-1922) designed his own approach to exploring the human psyche. After receiving his medical training, Rorschach began a study based upon a game he had played in childhood in which pictures were made through the use of inkblots. His study, "Psychodiagnostics" detailed how he had used inkblots to explore the unconscious minds of sane individuals as well as mental patients. Their differing personal responses to the exact same images told Rorschach something unique about each individual's unconscious. Apparently, images and symbols can bring to the conscious mind of the individual various associations that can be correlated with something about that person's inner self. A great deal of research into the nature of the unconscious mind has involved the exploration of dreams and their associated symbolism. Dream research received perhaps its greatest boost when in a 1953 article in the journal *Science*, Eugene Aserinsky and Nathaniel Kleitman of the University of Chicago, discussed their findings that REM (rapid eye movement) sleep was indicative of dream periods. The discovery led to countless additional scientific investigations exploring the same topic. Due to innumerable studies like these into the nature of the unconscious undertaken since the time of Freud, much of the scientific community now accepts the fact that there is much more to the human creature than that which can be divulged by the conscious mind.

These investigations by scientists, psychologists, and physicians have explored such topics as the nature of the self, the unconscious mind, dreams, and personal and archetypal (or universal) symbolism. Much of this work has become so widely known that today the names of Freud, Jung, and even Rorschach are household terms. However, most individuals remain completely unaware of the fact that an individual with no scientific or psychological training also explored in great detail these same subjects for decades; his name was Edgar Cayce.

Throughout his life, Edgar Cayce (1877-1945) displayed one of the most remarkable psychic talents of all time. Daily for over forty years of his adult life, Cayce was able to put himself into a deep state of relaxation and meditation. While in this sleep state, he was able to speak in a normal voice and give insightful answers to any question that he was asked. Rather than being the stuff of science fiction, the information he provided has proven so valuable that it has been repeatedly studied by educators, historians, theologians, medical professionals, and scientists the world over. The biographical details of Cayce's life and work can be found in such titles as *There Is a River* (1942) by Thomas Sugrue, *Many Mansions* (1950) by Gina Cerminara, and *Edgar Cayce: An American Prophet* (2000) by Sidney D. Kirkpatrick.

One of the most amazing things about the Cayce information is the vast scope of subject matter explored by his psychic readings. In fact, in areas of study such as history, medicine, holistic health, psychology, intuition, personal spirituality, and the nature of the mind, Edgar Cayce has repeatedly proven himself years ahead of his time as both science and history have frequently validated his information.

Echoing Carl Jung's call for the exploration of the unconscious mind, during the course of a 1924 reading given in Dayton, Ohio, Edgar Cayce stated that, "The study from the human standpoint, of subconscious, subliminal, psychic, soul forces, is and should be the great study for the human family . . . " (3744-5)[1] Cayce believed that such an undertaking would enable individuals to more fully come to know themselves. Rather than being an exercise in egotism, Cayce went on to explain his rationale: "When one understands self, and self's relation to its Maker, the duty to its neighbor, its own duty to self, it cannot, it will not be false to man, or to its Maker."

The Cayce material provides innumerable suggestions that individuals can utilize in order to more fully come to know themselves. These suggestions include such tools as meditation, the recording and analysis of personal dreams, working with spiritual ideals, music, art, drama, personal introspection and reflection, and developing an appreciation for the beauty of nature. Coming to know one's self was of such importance, Cayce told a small group of individuals involved in the study of personal spirituality that it was actually the second lesson (after cooperation) every individual should undertake for their own soul development (262-2).

For Cayce, one aspect of coming to know one's self was understanding how dreams and the corresponding symbols served as a reflection of the subconscious mind and its interrelationship with the physical, the mental, and the spiritual components of the individual:

As we see, all visions and dreams are given for the benefit

---

[1]During Cayce's life, the Edgar Cayce readings were all numbered to provide confidentiality. The first set of numbers (e.g., "3744") refers to the individual or group for whom the reading was given. The second set of numbers (e.g., "5") refers to the number in the series from which the reading is taken. For example, 3744-5 identifies the reading as the fifth one given to the subject assigned #3744.

of the individual, would they but interpret them correctly, for we find that visions, or dreams, in whatever character they may come, are the reflection, either of the physical condition, with apparitions with same, or of the subconscious, with the conditions relating to the physical body and its action, either through mental or through the elements of the spiritual entity, or a projection from the spiritual forces to the subconscious of the individual, and happy may he be that is able to say they have been spoken to through the dream or vision.   294-15

At a time when dream study was, for the most part, being used only in psychology and psychoanalysis, the Cayce readings were encouraging regular individuals: housewives, husbands, students, business people, fathers and mothers, and children to work with their dreams as a means of better understanding themselves and their relationships with others. Hundreds of Edgar Cayce readings discuss the meaning of dreams and the analysis of dream symbols.

In addition to dreams, there is actually a wealth of information found in the Edgar Cayce material dealing with the interpretation of personal symbolism. That information relates specifically to three important tools the readings recommended for coming to know one's self: the use of life seals, the creation of an aura chart and the study of the Book of Revelation.

Essentially, both life seals and aura charts are visual drawings and artistic depictions of symbols and images that can assist the individual in better understanding him or herself. In regards to the Book of Revelation, Cayce believed that it was primarily a symbolic representation of what transpires within an individual as consciousness expands and spiritual development begin to take place. From Cayce's perspective, each of these tools would be invaluable for any individual interested in personal and spiritual growth, soul development, life direction, soul memory, transformational consciousness, self-awareness, cultivating talents, overcoming faults and weaknesses, or working with personal symbolism.

Life seals are simply drawings individuals usually create within a circle that help them to better understand themselves. The drawings contain pictures and images that have a symbolic importance to the individual. Ultimately, these seals serve as reminders of a person's talents as well as those things that the individual may need to be working on in the present. In 1933, Cayce told a twenty-year-old woman that she had the ability to create life seals for others. Describing the purpose of these drawings, he stated:

> . . . that which will arouse in the inner self of individuals, individual minds, individual souls, that which will aid those individuals in knowing themselves, their weaknesses, their faults, their uprisings, their downsittings. That which enables the individual soul to see itself better. And that which aids each individual or hinders it, or is helpful to it in giving expression of itself in the present experience. 275-36

Interestingly enough, the Cayce information on life seals presents an amazing similarity to Carl Jung's information on the use of mandalas. In Jung's case, for about ten years starting in 1918 he began to sketch a series of circular drawings every morning that seemed to reflect his inner situation and experience. He called each of these drawings a mandala–the Sanskrit word for circle–and he eventually realized how these drawings seemed to be reflective of his own subjective thought processes, presenting an objective look at his psyche:

> My mandalas were cryptograms concerning the state of self which were presented to me anew each day. In them I saw the self–that is, my whole being–actively at work. To be sure, at first I could only dimly understand them; but they seemed to me highly significant, and I guarded them like precious pearls. I had the distinct feeling that they were something central, and in time I acquired through them a living conception of the self . . .
> It became increasingly clear to me that the mandala is the center. It is the exponent of all paths. It is the path to

the center, to individuation . . . I knew that in finding the mandala as an expression of the self I had attained what was for me the ultimate. (Jung, *Memories, Dreams, Reflections*, pgs. 196-197)

Educator, activist, author, and art historian, José Argüelles, would later say of the mandala:

It is a natural form, often reproduced spontaneously when the restrictive workings of consciousness do not impede the flow of the unconscious. Moreover, the mandala is a prime tool for self-integration; the creation of a mandala signals the reorganization of the various components of personality to reach a new level of stability—and perhaps even a new personality. (Argüelles, pg. 199)

Building upon the use of personal symbolism as a means of understanding the self while also incorporating the concepts of reincarnation and soul memory, the Edgar Cayce readings recommended the creation of what he called an Aura Chart. The aura chart is a visual depiction of a soul's journey with pictures, images, and symbols that portray what that soul has learned as well as where it has succeeded and where it has failed in its passage through time. The aura chart depicts those lifetimes/incarnations that are most influencing the individual in the present–in other words those periods in history to which the individuals feels most drawn and has the greatest emotional response (good or bad). Essentially, the aura chart is simply a visual representation of what Cayce referred to as the soul's Akashic Record: the universal record or database of each individual's personal soul journey.

In 1942, a thirty-one-year-old auto salesman who had requested an aura chart for himself was told of its purpose:

In giving an aura chart–this we would indicate as to the high points in the experiences of the entity in the earth, having to do with the manner in which the entity has conducted or is conducting itself in the present for the greater unfoldment—spiritually, mentally and materially . . .

The beauty of such a drawing depends much upon the concept of the artist. Yet these may visualize for the entity that as may bring helpful influences into the experience.

533-20

In 1946, the year after Cayce's death, psychologist Dr. Gina Cerminara wrote a brief article on aura charts and described her perception of their eventual importance, as follows:

Once reincarnation is widely accepted by psychologists, it will be found valuable to have some symbolic means of recalling to mind, and keeping present in consciousness, the major purpose of the present incarnation. Inasmuch as the purpose of any single incarnation is intimately bound up with the lives which have preceded it, the aura charts that Mr. Cayce gave seem to presage one method, at least, of achieving just such a visual reminder. (Cerminara, "Archetypes and Aura Charts," pg. 3)

Dr. Cerminara went out to say that once individuals realized how aura charts (as well as life seals) could be utilized to lead to "an inner life of ever-expanding awareness," even individuals who had never had a psychic reading as well as those who were unaware of their past lives could create their own charts and seals. In this regard she suggested that individuals simply work with their intuition and creativity and choose symbols that represented both qualities and circumstances they wished to make manifest in their lives.

The idea of using symbolism to facilitate personal growth and expanding consciousness as well as a means of understanding one's inner self is connected to what transpires during the Jungian concept of individuation. Essentially, the process of individuation is one in which the conscious mind comes to terms with its inner Self, integrates the substance of the unconscious, and gradually journeys toward personal wholeness. This disconnected nature of the human creature on its journey toward wholeness is often depicted in archetypal imagery, symbolism, dreams, visions, as well as fairy tales and myths. For example, although children's classics such as the *Wizard of Oz* and *Pinocchio* might be read as nothing more than entertaining stories, both are actually symbolic of the soul's journey toward personal wholeness and enlightenment.

Even the word "symbol" is somehow associated with he idea of wholeness. The word is actually derived from the Greek word "symbolon." In ancient Greece it was customary to break a slate of burned clay into several pieces and distribute those pieces among individuals who belonged to a specific group. The broken piece possessed by each individual was called a symbolon. When the group reunited, the pieces were fit back together to verify the bearer's identity and thereby confirm that each individual was truly a member of that group.

Conflicting with the ideas of individuation and wholeness, Carl Jung stated that it was all too common for the contemporary world to overlook the importance of religious symbols and spiritual meaning in everyday life. When asked why God did not seem to speak to the modern world as He reportedly did in days gone by, Jung replied: "We are so captivated by and entangled in our subjective consciousness that we have forgotten the age-old fact that God speaks chiefly through visions and dreams." (Jung, *Man and His Symbols,* pg. 92) Cayce repeatedly confirmed this same idea and once assured a forty-one-year-old Jewish businessman that even in the contemporary world God still desired to both assist and warn individuals in their activities in everyday life through dreams and visions (257-138).

In terms of religious symbolism and its importance to individuals, the greatest source of analysis and exploration ever undertaken by the Edgar Cayce readings is perhaps the Book of Revelation–the last chapter in the Bible, which is generally believed to have been compiled by the Apostle John. Historically, John's experience of the Revelation occurred while he was in exile on the island of Patmos. According to Cayce, the Revelation contains a series of images, symbols, and visions corresponding to John's awakening to higher states of consciousness and the pattern of wholeness within himself. These symbols correspond to archetypal patterns within all individuals and are brought to conscious awareness in dreams, visions, and personal revelation as individuals make progress in their own spiritual development.

Much of the Revelation's imagery is associated not with external prophecy and world affairs (as many believe) but rather with the internal struggles and "warring" within an individual that takes place as the various parts of the self move toward spiritual awakening and wholeness. According to Cayce:

> For the visions, the experiences, the names, the churches, the places, the dragons, the cities, all are but emblems of those forces that may war within the individual in its journey through the material, or from the entering into the material manifestation to the entering into the glory, or the awakening in the spirit, in the inter-between, in the borderland, in the shadow. 281-16

Associated with this same idea, Carl Jung frequently stated that the images of the four creatures (the ox, the eagle, the lion, and the man) that could be found in Ezekiel and the Revelation were psychologically "a symbol of the self." (Jung, *Collected Works, 14,* 269) For Jung, these images could be correlated with unconscious states within each individual and correspond to various levels of development.

Frequently, the Cayce readings recommended Revelation as a tool for understanding the self. On one occasion, Edgar Cayce told a chiropractor interested in psychoanalysis that the real motivating forces within the physical body were the connections and coordination between the central nervous system and the cerebrospinal system. In order to better understand these connections it was recommended that the chiropractor study the Revelation: "For if you will read the Book of Revelation with the idea of the body as the interpretation, you will understand yourself and learn to really analyze, psychoanalyze, mentally analyze others." (4083-1) Cayce's sense of the importance of Revelation is evident by the fact that more than two hundred readings reference some portion of the Book of Revelation and twenty-three examine John's experience in great detail.

Rather than seeing the exploration of symbolism as an end unto itself, the Edgar Cayce readings suggest that symbols, signs, and vibrations are essentially guiding lights or signposts along the way. In the language of the readings, "These are but lights, but signs in thine experience, they are as but a candle that one stumbles not in the dark." (707-2) In other words, they are essentially tools that can enable individuals to find themselves as well as their direction in life.

With that in mind, this book was written in an effort to help individuals understand the nature of personal symbolism and how it might be useful in their own journeys toward wholeness. Each of us, regardless of whom or where we might be, are on a life journey. Ultimately, the journey is a purposeful one of experiences and relationships, enabling each of us to discover who we are. To some, the journey appears to be filled with material goals, accomplishments, successes and failures. Others measure that journey by milestones–good or bad. Only a few seem to hold the awareness that the journey is ultimately one of self-discovery and personal enlightenment. Regardless of the varying perceptions, on this journey all are seekers–some seeking sustenance and the appeasement of needs; some seeking aspirations and dreams; some in search of something they cannot quite describe other than by their sense of its lack. The ultimate certainty of the journey, however, is that it is essentially a search for one's Self.

Part One: Life Seals

At last the large egg broke, and a young one crept forth crying, "Peep, peep." It was very large and ugly. The duck stared at it and exclaimed, "It is very large and not at all like the others. I wonder if it really is a turkey . . . "

"Let him alone," said the mother; "he is not doing any harm."

"Yes, but he is so big and ugly," said the spiteful duck "and therefore he must be turned out."

"The others are very pretty children," said the old duck, with the rag on her leg, "all but that one; I wish his mother could improve him a little."

"That is impossible, your grace," replied the mother; "he is not pretty; but he has a very good disposition, and swims as well or even better than the others. I think he will grow up pretty, and perhaps be smaller; he has remained too long in the egg, and therefore his figure is not properly formed;" and then she stroked his neck and smoothed the feathers, saying, "It is a drake, and therefore not of so much consequence. I think he will grow up strong, and able to take care of himself."

Excerpt from The Ugly Duckling
Hans Christian Andersen, 1844

1

The Life Seal as a Tool for Self-Awareness

In terms of exploring the importance of personal symbolism, the Edgar Cayce readings contain approximately 150 references to life seals[2]. Essentially, a life seal is an artistic depiction of symbols that can assist an individual in remembering her or his talents or present purposes. It is a symbolic reminder of what the individual is ultimately trying to accomplish at a soul level. From this perspective, some seals might focus on a quality that needs to be further developed, while others could represent a trait that needs to be rooted out of the individual's consciousness. With this in mind, each individual might depict her or his life seal in a number of different ways as well as with a variety of symbols at any point in life.

---

[2]When referring to life seals, the readings use various terms to describe the same thing, including Seal of Life, Symbol of Life, Patterns, Pattern of Life, Emblems and Emblem of Life.

Primarily, life seals are to be used for personal motivation. They are designed to remind an individual's subconscious mind of past experiences or particular lessons. Because of the personal nature of life seals their meaning is specific to the individual. In other words, two people might create very similar looking life seals, but because of personal associations with the symbols and images, the seal could have very different meanings for each individual.

The readings suggest that life seals were frequently used in ancient Egypt as a source of personal understanding and guidance and could serve the very same function in the present. For example, an individual might decide to create a life seal as a drawing or a painting and then study that seal each morning and evening when analyzing the day's events and the experiences he or she had with others. In this regard a life seal might be something you look at upon awakening to remind you of why you are here and again at night to reflect upon how well you did in fulfilling what you hoped to accomplish. Consisting of only a few symbols, life seals can be described as a material representation of a past experience, an important direction, or a soul reminder. They can be most helpful in calling to mind an individual's present purposes.

Individuals who received readings from Edgar Cayce sometimes specifically requested information on life seals but–as if to confirm the benefit of working with this type of personal symbolism–the information was often volunteered during the course of a reading regardless of the reading's primary topic. Sometimes, however, when individuals requested that Edgar Cayce describe what their seal might look like, he responded by stating that the creation of a life seal was something that might best be done from within themselves (845-1 and others). In other words, the symbols could be drawn out from their own subconscious mind.

In order to create a personal life seal, individuals were often told to take a piece of paper or white cardboard, somewhere between fourteen and eighteen inches square, and to draw a circle on that cardboard, generally between twelve and thirteen inches in diameter. Sometimes the directions were given somewhat differently for each individual. For example, Ms. [2448], a twenty-five-year-old bookkeeper was told that her life seal might best be drawn in the shape of a scroll. On another occasion, a thirty-seven-year-old woman who had already encountered a variety of life events, including motherhood, divorce, and running a small boardinghouse was instructed to make her seal in the shape of an eight-sided circle (octagon) as a means of symbolizing the various aspects of her life (3637-1). Sometimes other individuals were told that they might decide to make their life seals in the shape of a shield, a plaque, or an oval. Once an individual was even told that a square would be an appropriate shape because the reading described the person as "a square-shooter." (3418-1) Most often, however, the shape of a circle was recommended, symbolizing the self, and the symbols and images were to be placed within the boundaries of that circle.

Perhaps surprisingly, the first use of a life seal in the Edgar Cayce work occurred somewhat accidentally. In 1926, a twenty-two-year-old woman who had become friends with Cayce's eldest son, Hugh Lynn, volunteered to sketch the cover of a booklet regarding Edgar Cayce's work that was being prepared as an introduction for new people. As background information, the young woman was apparently told that throughout his life Edgar Cayce had often dreamed of the image of a desert well surrounded by three palm trees. In addition to the dream image, she was given information about Cayce's personal psychic experiences as well as what the readings had said about his own past-life experiences. According to the readings, important past-life experiences had included ancient Egypt, ancient Persia, and Palestine. It was during his lifetime in Persia that Cayce had reportedly been mortally wounded and had undergone an out-of-body experience–somehow being able to heal himself. The readings suggested that this experience in being separated from his physical body had forever enhanced his psychic abilities.

Drawing upon this past-life information, Edgar Cayce's dreams, and the background material provided in the introductory booklet, Miss [2486] sketched the cover of the introductory booklet.

See Edgar Cayce's Life Seal—Image 1: Painted by Miss [2486]—at the end of Chapter Three.

Edgar Cayce was so pleased with the young woman's drawing that he offered to give her a "life reading" in exchange for her work and expressed his gratitude in a letter dated March 10, 1926:

> Dear Miss [2486]:
> I want to thank you and assure you of my appreciation of
> your so kindly attempting to make this sketch for me, that
> has been a dream with me for a long time, and then to
> find it so wonderfully executed, even in a way that I don't
> think to my own mind could be better improved upon, is
> certainly most gratifying . . .

Thereafter, the booklet was called "the Cayce Introductory Booklet."

After the sketch by Miss [2486] was drawn, the first two intentional references to the subject of life seals did not occur for another four years. The first reference was given to a Jewish housewife and the second was given to a Protestant bank executive.

In May of 1930, the forty-three-year-old housewife requested information about her soul's history, lessons, and experiences in the form of a Cayce life reading, dealing with the subject of reincarnation. During the course of the reading the woman was informed that her greatest talent in the present was in the field of artistic writing, specifically in terms of history or drama. One of the strongest influences from her soul's past had occurred in France during the time of Louis XIV and Louis XV when she had been acquainted with the French royal family. During that period she had apparently risen from a position of obscurity to one of stature in which she had developed the ability to lead others. Cayce suggested that she adopt the "fleur de lis" (the coat of arms resembling the lily that had once belonged to French royal family) as her personal emblem. The rationale was that it would help her call to mind some of the innate abilities and strengths acquired in the past that could be beneficial to her in the present (2541-3). The woman was even encouraged to wear the fleur de lis as a pin and to occasionally wear attire that incorporated the image of the flower into the design of her clothing.

The second life seal reference occurred in December of that same year during a life reading given to a forty-three-year-old banker (261-5). While tracing the past lives and the individual's abilities in finance, diplomacy, and politics, Cayce mentioned that the banker was also gifted in the arts and had an appreciation for design, mosaics, and architecture. The reading went on to state that during a past life in Egypt, Mr. [261] had apparently created life seals for individuals and that the seals he had created for himself as well as for one of the kings of the period continued to exist (although as yet undiscovered) in the Egyptian desert.

Although it was not realized at the time, a third important event occurred in 1930 that would eventually provide Cayce's contemporaries with a great deal of information on the subject of life seals. In March of that year parents of a seventeen-year-old girl brought their daughter, Margret Zentgraf, to the Cayce Hospital for treatment. Her condition had been diagnosed as erosion of the femur bone, causing her a great deal of pain. Some feared that the condition was precancerous and could only deteriorate. Doctor's had wanted to perform experimental surgery, although admitting that the surgery might cripple the young woman permanently. Rather than pursuing the surgery, Margret's parents brought her to Edgar Cayce.

The readings' recommendations included physiotherapy, osteopathic adjustments, medication, gentle exercise, and electrotherapy. After she began the treatments, both the pain and the inflammation began to heal, and Margret's condition improved dramatically. So impressed were the Zentgrafs with the Cayce diagnosis and treatment that eventually they obtained life readings for themselves and every member of their family.

Margret received her life reading in October 1930. Cayce described innate talents as both a dietician and a harpist–skills that she had apparently acquired during an incarnation in ancient Egypt. She was also told that she had worked in the Egyptian temples and had been instrumental in assisting individuals in getting in touch with their own life's direction and purpose. Cayce advised her to work with music and personal attunement so that she could again draw upon the same qualities and abilities she had once demonstrated in Egypt.

Following the reading's advice, within a few years Margret had become quite skilled at playing the harp. She had also begun to work with meditation and had greatly enhanced her own intuition. It was while she worked with meditation that she began receiving in her mind's eye the image of life seals for other people. Follow-up readings given in 1933 explained that her ability to create life seals was actually one of those talents she had developed as a musician and counselor during her Egyptian incarnation. During that lifetime, her work with life seals had helped individuals in understanding themselves and their relationship to the whole.

Cayce informed her that when she created a life seal in the present it would have the same effect and that it would "arouse within the individual the *desire* to seek to know *self*." Once this occurred, individuals would seek to know their relationship to God and soul development would occur as a natural result. The reading told Margret that her life seals would have such an impact upon the individual for whom it was created that the person would be "in awe." (275-35)

Working with meditation and her own creativity, Margret Zentgraf began making life seals for her family and a large number of friends and associates. In September 1933, she sent members of the Cayce family a booklet containing their life seals and her interpretation. So amazed was Edgar Cayce by her work that he wrote Margret's mother on September 27, 1933, and Margret two weeks later:

September 27, 1933

Dear [Mrs. Zentgraf]:

> I have received the book of seals [done by Margret], and am just amazed. I will try and write Margret as soon as have the opportunity to assimilate something of the beauty and wonder presented in these. The execution is so WONDERFUL. And the symbols just put me in such awe, it's hard to find words to express how I feel . . .

October 9, 1933

Dear Margret:

> . . . I have been trying to find the right words to express my appreciation, and at the same time to give some idea of how wonderful I think the book [of seals] is that you sent me. Yet I find myself almost awe-inspired by the visions that keep crowding in, as I look over these pages [of seals and their interpretations] from time to time, until I

have no words even to begin to convey what I think and feel about them. Possibly when I can sit down and talk with you and the others whom I'm sure your work has inspired also, I may give expression to something of what it has been worth to me. The seals are not only remarkable; they are really inspiring, and to my mind they carry a picture of each soul's development; needs, faults, desires; in fact, the whole life, to which these seals appear to be the key. To be sure, it will require thought and study on the part of each one to open the door to that expressed in the seals, for his own development. For, after all, it is ALL self-development. And in the correct expression of self, that which is given out raises those whom the entity or soul contacts . . . I hope that we may be able to talk these things over together. I'm sure each individual will be the best interpreter of his own seal, as life begins to unfold for him.

Thank you a thousand times for the consideration you have given me in preparing the book and sending it to me. I will bring it with me, so that we can discuss it.

With love and regards to each and every one from all here, I am

Sincerely, Edgar Cayce

275-11 Reports

When creating Edgar Cayce's life seal, Margret began with the seal created by Ms. [2486] four years earlier but incorporated changes of her own.

Edgar Cayce's Life Seal
Image 2: Painted by Margret Zentgraf

Previously, Margret had described her sense of what the symbols in Cayce's seal meant, as well as why changes needed to be made to the original 1926 version:

The pyramid represents the Egyptian life. The well the Persian life; the trees the trinity of Christ, the Savior, Leader, Brother. The swans represent the other lives that were of no importance to complete the seal of life. The sailboat means the age of psychic knowledge which we are entering. The cross brings the religious element in, which is very important. Radiating, because through his power will, has and is, bringing peace, joy, and harmony to many. Of course healing through the physical readings.

[In regards to correcting some elements of the first version of Cayce's life seal.] The sailboat should be larger, much larger, as that is very important; the swans are all right except they could be made a little more perfectly. The birds are all right, but really take away from the effect. The palm trees and well could be a little larger too, and the sun of course equal to them. The word "Cayce" really should not be on it, because it is not really bringing anything to him that will inspire him. And since that is the object of all of the seals, it would be better to leave it out. In its place put a cross; it will only be a small one, but very important.

[In regards to the suggested colors.] The outside ring gold, the sun and rays gold, the pyramid gold, the cross and rays gold; the sailboat black and the sail white, the water blue, but only make the small lines, not solid. The swans white with black lines, and the water blue; the cloud white and gold. The palm trees green, with gold trunks; the well black with gold lines, the grass green. The line of the desert make gold. Leave the rest gray, the color of the paper.   294-8 Reports

In 1934 Margret Zentgraf put together a small booklet entitled *Seals*, describing her work with life seals. Her booklet offered to make seals available to other people for a suggested contribution of $10. As other individuals began to know about the possibility of having a life seal for themselves, they began making requests for the information in their own readings. According to a file notation from January 1935 made by Edgar Cayce's secretary, Gladys Davis, the head of the A.R.E. Study Group work, Esther Wynne, had suggested that because of the importance of personal symbolism a standard question for each life reading should include the following: "What is my seal, to what color or colors do I best vibrate, and what is my musical note?" (797-1) The readings themselves also started to volunteer the information regarding personal life seals with greater frequency.

Because life seals provide individuals with personal and vocational direction, it was not unusual for parents to request and/or receive the information about seals from Edgar Cayce for their children. For example, parents of a five-year-old girl were told that their child's talents were in the field of interior decorating and design. For that reason, they were encouraged to have a life seal created for the child that included a background of floral designs. Because the little girl was also prone to being out of control, Cayce advised placing the picture of an out-of-control automobile in the seal as a symbolic reminder of the tendency that she needed to overcome (1635-3). (For an examination and interpretation of over 300 symbols refer to the Appendix.)

On another occasion, it was suggested that the life seal for an eight-year-old girl contain two images that represented a significant choice that she would be faced with in the present. One of the images was of a honeybee, which apparently represented the possibility of being fruitful and productive in her activities and associations with others. The other image was of a bumblebee, which indicated the possibility of fleeing from creative endeavors and positive associations with others. Cayce stated that in this manner the child's life seal would include warnings to assist them in directing and encouraging their daughter. He went on to advise, "For remember, as given, train the child in the way it should go, and when it is old it will not depart from it." (3621-1)

Parents of a two-year-old boy were told that their child's future would be in the field of global communications. They were encouraged to incorporate "in miniature" symbols or pictures of those portions of the globe that were destined to be a part of their child's future, including: Moscow, Greenwich, Ankara, Baghdad, Buenos Aires, Lima, and Auckland (2542-1). Various symbols given to other children to be used in the creation of their own life seals were as follows:

An eleven-year-old girl with innate talents for the arts, music, and drama was told that her life seal should contain a picture of "the harp or the horn"–instruments that could become a part of her life experience in the present (405-1).

An eighteen-year-old boy, who was told that his greatest life's work could be in the direction of providing vocational guidance to others, was instructed that the symbol of a compass should be included in his life seal (797-1).

Parents of a four-year-old boy with innate talents as an orator, lawyer, and minister were told that their son's life seal should contain symbols that could call to mind each of these professions (415-1).

As in the case of adults, children were supposed to be able to see their life seals regularly as a means of reminding them at a subconscious level of their soul talents, abilities, shortcomings, and direction. Even seeing the symbols, the colors or the pictures used within the life seal was somehow supposed to be helpful. One example reported in the Cayce files concerns the case of a three-year-old girl, whose grandmother was told that the child would be positively influenced by the color purple. It was suggested that a life seal be created that contained, in part, the color purple.

After receiving the child's reading, the grandmother reported an experience that seemed to confirm Cayce's information. One day the child had been in the throes of being cross, temperamental, and angry. Nothing had seemed to be able to appease the girl and finally–not knowing what else to do–the grandmother remembered how purple was supposed to be helpful to the child. Since the life seal had not yet been created and since she did not have anything else that was colored purple, the grandmother hung one of her own purple dresses in the child's room. Almost immediately the little girl became more relaxed, her anger disappeared, and the grandmother reported that she had no more trouble with the child for the rest of the day (324-5).

The symbolic importance of vocational direction was not limited to life seals for children. Even adults who were well established in their careers or in fulfilling their life's mission were encouraged to incorporate symbols that would illustrate those abilities in the creation of their life seals. For example, the life seal of a forty-five-year-old nurse was to include the picture of a nurse and a patient, symbolizing the woman's service and healing abilities (3908-1). On another occasion, a forty-five-year-old woman who worked with prayer and spiritual healing was told to include a bell in her life seal, indicating her talent for sending out messages of help, aid, and higher energy through prayer to others (993-4). The life seal of a twenty-year-old woman was to include a picture of the emanations from the rays of the sun, symbolizing her ability to guide individuals by example to finding the hopefulness of their own personal ideals (562-3).

For a fifty-four-year-old housewife who possessed an enthusiasm for "other cities," "other places," and "other lands," Cayce encouraged her to utilize the picture of the earth in her life seal. Because she was also positively affected by the scent of lavender, it was suggested that a picture of the plant be a portion of her seal, as well (379-3). A woman whose talents were in the direction of working with children was encouraged to put "children of all status of development" into her seal (3474-1).

In addition to present-life motivational symbols, it was not uncommon for individuals to be advised to utilize symbols in their life seals that were most associated with their soul's past. People who were drawn, for example, to various cultures from the past, such as Roman, Palestinian, or Egyptian were often advised to include Latin phrases, Hebrew words or Egyptian hieroglyphics, respectively, in their seals (910-4, 259-8, 601-5, 2305-2, 2448-2, and others). Another means of depicting influential periods from history that had been a part of a soul's past included the use of pyramids, columns, and even mountain ranges that corresponded to such places as Atlantis, Egypt, Persia, and Palestine (1610-2, 2390-1, 845-1, 603-2, and others).

Individuals who had been working in the past with spiritual principles, had been Crusaders of Christian ideals, or had personal past-life experiences at the time of Jesus, were frequently encouraged to put the symbol of a cross, a lamb, or the image of Jesus in their life seals (3637-1, 2454-3, 1825-1, 3037-1, 845-1, and others).

Other examples of past-life symbols include the case of a forty-four-year-old housewife who had experienced a number of disappointments in former lifetimes because of her home life. She was encouraged to put the picture of home and a disappointed individual leaving the home in her seal as a reminder of those experiences (2519-8). A woman whose past lives had included experiences with spiritual leaders, as a member of royalty, and working with healing was encouraged to use the following colors in the creation of her life seal: white for purity, purple for royalty, and green for healing (1223-4). A woman who was drawn to nature and crops in the field was told that she had encountered a past life in which she had worked in a granary, milling wheat for food. An appropriate life seal symbol for her included the picture of a woman in the field with a sickle (808-18).

Symbols of nature, such as trees, flowers, and animals, were often suggested for use in the creation of a life seal. The depiction of flowers, blooms, or berries symbolized such things as talents, abilities, beauty, and growth (1788-3, 1775-1, 2285-1, 1958-1, 3091-1, 2946-2, 2308-1, and others). An individual who was drawn to frequently seeking new knowledge that sprang to life was counseled to incorporate blades of grass in the foreground of her personal seal (2390-1). Another woman who was encouraged to draw upon the latent knowledge and abilities that she possessed within herself was told to place a book in the center of her life seal. She was also encouraged to include a rose and a bee in the seal, indicating her appreciation for the beauty and sweetness of life (in terms of the rose) and her talent for making productive associations with others (corresponding to the bee) (2376-4).

A twenty-one-year-old woman who wanted to know how best to fulfill her purpose in life and to become of greater service to others was told to work with her life seal. She was encouraged to use the seal as a focal point, representing her purpose, and to reflect upon it as a means of making choices in her life (1981-2).

Since the purpose of the symbols chosen for an individual life seal were specifically to resonate to something within an individual's own subconscious mind, anything imaginable might become part of a personal seal. In the case of a thirty-four-year-old man who was "mechanically minded," the design of his life seal was to include the symbol of a wheel in motion (2385-1). One individual was encouraged to put the image of a fallen stump covered with flowers in her life

seal, symbolizing the strength and beauty of a life well lived (1775-1).
The seal given for a forty-year-old art teacher in 1943 contained many more than the three to eight symbols normally described. In addition to being a teacher, mother, and housewife, she possessed musical talents, loved to learn, and enjoyed various aspects of her home life. Cayce detailed her life seal, as follows:

> Put in the lower right hand corner the staff–of music and bars on same–the symbols for this; indicating the musical talents of the entity, interests in same but at extremes, see?
>
> In the lower left hand corner put a book, an open page, with flowers–cut flowers–laid across the open page–at least three roses, red, yellow, white, with a sprig of maiden hair fern; these signifying the experiences of the entity in the earth.
>
> In the upper right hand corner put the interior of a room–chair, lamp, window, cat, dog, and a sewing basket, but no figure–other than the animal in the chair. The room should show light coming from the window, before which these articles would be set; the dog upon the floor looking at the window, the cat curled in the chair; all of these being the symbols for the domestic experiences through the sojourns and the extremes to which the entity has gone, and those tendencies in the present experiences.
>
> 3407-1

When the woman asked toward the end of her reading, "What was the purpose of my entering the earth's plane at this time?" Cayce replied simply, "To complete self's finding self."

On a number of occasions, words that expressed traits or qualities that needed to become a portion of the individual's life were encouraged to be literally written within a person's seal. For example, some individuals were told to write words such as "patience," "love," "persistence," "kindness," and even "I believe" into the seal itself (1688-6, 3691-1, 3051-2 and others).

Those who had been warriors for truth or had literal past-life experiences in battle might be told to incorporate the symbol of a helmet, a shield, or a battle-ax in their seals (2173-1, 984-1, 1635-3, 1859-1, 1223-4, and others). Anything that could symbolize something important to the individual was an appropriate image for the creation of a life seal.

In addition to symbols and words, the importance of such things as colors, numbers, and even planetary symbols could be an aspect of life seals described in the Cayce readings. For example, green could be utilized to emphasize healing or growth and white might be associated with purity, service, or the white light of the divine (3091-1 and 3908-1, respectively). In terms of astrological influences, Mercury was used to emphasize the mind or mental influences (2683-1) and Uranus was associated with moods or being prone to extremes (3407-1). Numbers of objects or lines had their corresponding meaning, as well. For example, one individual was encouraged to utilize three lines in her life seal, symbolizing the three phases of human experience: physical, mental, and spiritual (3051-2). Another individual was told that the life seal should contain a drawing of four spokes of a wheel, corresponding to four traits that needed to be personally cultivated (1688-6).

In 1939, Cayce told a beauty salon manager that the symbols within a life seal were drawn from a variety of different approaches. These included: important astrological influences, past-life experiences of the individual, patterns in the person's life experiences, as well as representations of various choices and decisions that had been made in relationship to people, things, and conditions. The same woman was advised to take the time to draw her seal because in the very process of doing so she would gain an awareness of her relationship to self as well as her connection to God (1825-1).

A thirty-one-year-old housewife was encouraged to reflect upon memories and places that reminded her of her life's experiences when pulling together images and symbols for her own life seal (2072-4). Even dreams presented the appropriate impulse for life seal images, as in the case of a forty-eight-year-old woman who was told that the outstanding symbols she had received in her dreams should become a part of her seal (5373-1).

When a fifty-six-year-old astrologer received the description of her life seal, Cayce encouraged her to use it as a tool for visualization that would enable her to discern the answer to different questions that arose in her life. From this perspective, Cayce stated, "It is *not* as a motive for meditation . . . rather as the answer in meditation." (2880-2) Along the same lines, a fifty-year-old widow was encouraged to work with her life seal as "something to be studied each morning or evening when ye would analyze thyself and the motives of others." (1770-3)

Essentially, the readings advised people to work with life seals as a reminder and a motivator for personal growth and development. By working with this tool of personal symbolism, individuals were encouraged that they would be provided with a means of making decisions, a method of coming to know themselves, and yet one more approach to cultivating an awareness of their relationship with the divine.

Edgar Cayce, who died in 1945, continued to provide information on life seals for as long as he gave readings, through much of 1944. Margret Zentgraf, however, apparently stopped working with life seals in the late 1930s. According to the Cayce files, in 1938, Margret's family had to move to Germany in order to collect an inheritance that belonged to her mother. Because of conflicts throughout Europe and the outbreak of World War II, the family was not able to return to the United States until 1946. Although for a time things went well enough for the family in Germany, the war had a devastating effect on their ability to get food, clothing, and proper medical treatment. In fact, in 1943 Edgar Cayce had a dream about Margret and upon awakening noted that he had never seen "Margret look so emaciated." (275-36 Reports)

A few years after the family returned to the United States, Margret and her sister opened up a nursery school and kindergarten. The two young women also pursued their love of music and became part of the symphony orchestra. By 1975 they had become well known performing artists. Margret's physical condition, however, deteriorated and she was forced to undergo a series of surgeries and physical therapies in order to help correct ongoing problems with her hip and spine. She never fully recovered and family members traced her health problems to their inability to receive proper food and medical treatment during the war years. Margret passed away at the age of eighty in 1992. According to notations within the Cayce files, after the family had gone to Germany, she never again attempted to work with life seals. Her influence on the Cayce readings and life seals, however, should not be underestimated.

Essentially, a life seal can be used as a valuable tool for personal motivation. Cayce believed that these seals could be helpful for individuals in terms of self-awareness, personal direction, cultivating talents, and overcoming faults and weaknesses. When someone creates a personal seal, it serves as a means of eliciting from within the individual information about the Self and Self's connection to the divine.

Reflecting upon a life seal is also a way of speaking to the unconscious directly. A seal suggests that what you are in the present is the sum of what you apply in your daily experience. The symbols generally have a meaning specifically important to the individual. Ultimately, from the perspective of the Edgar Cayce information, life seals are essentially tools for coming to know one's self. That self-knowledge occurs whether it's discovering one's inner qualities, calling to mind a trait that needs to be overcome, providing guidance and direction, or motivating an individual to become all that he or she was meant to be.

2

Exploring the
Symbolism of Life Seals

When Edgar Cayce gave a reading providing symbols that could be useful in the creation of a life seal, he was not choosing something outside of the individual that she or he was somehow supposed to accomplish. Instead, these symbols were pulled out of the individual's own consciousness and experience. The symbols would have a personal meaning to the individual while somehow calling forth from within that person the motivation to hold fast to the soul's highest purposes and ultimate desires. Margret Zentgraf's work with meditation and life seals allowed her to accomplish the same thing. Cayce described Margret's ability as follows:

> . . . that which will arouse within the individual the *desire* to seek to know *self*.   275-35

> . . . those abilities for the body to so visualize . . . that
> which will aid those individuals in knowing themselves . . .
> That which enables the individual soul to see itself better.
> And that which aids each individual or hinders it, or is
> helpful to it in giving expression of itself in the present
> experience . . .
>
> Hence the ability in the present to visualize,
> pictorialize, draw together, that which awakens something
> in the inner soul of those whom the entity *did* contact–
> and again contacts . . .   275-36

With the above in mind, it's important to remember that the meaning of personal symbols which are part of an individual's life seal are not affected by what anyone else might think about those same symbols. The symbols have a motivational influence that may not be understandable to others, just as a personal and contemporary life seal created by an individual for himself or herself in the present would not necessarily have the same impact on anyone else.

As a means of familiarizing individuals with the appearance of a variety of life seals and their corresponding interpretation, a number of seals from the Cayce files have been included. Each of the following life seals provides some background information on the person to whom the seal belonged, as well as an interpretation of what the pictures and images may have meant to that individual. (Note: The overall shape of the majority of life seals is that of a circle–suggestive of the self and all that is contained within the self.)

Margret Zentgraf's Personal Life Seal
Image 3: Drawn by herself

BACKGROUND: Margret Zentgraf was seventeen years old when she had her first reading for a physical condition in 1930. She was admitted to the Cayce hospital for treatment that same year. In time, she would obtain a life reading in which Edgar Cayce described how she could access talents and abilities she had originally acquired in ancient Egypt. It was later discovered that one of those abilities pertained to her ability to meditate and visualize life seals for other individuals. Margret Zentgraf created many of the life seals that continue to exist in the Cayce archives.

INTERPRETATION OF LIFE SEAL: The central picture is that of a lyre, a small harp used by the ancient Greeks. In addition to using the harp as a means of facilitating healing for others in ancient Egypt, Margret was told that one of her purposes in this life was to work with the harp. Music would, in fact, become a major influence for her throughout the rest of her life.

According to Margret, "The bow and arrow represent the age of healing through music, in that the music shoots out the sickness of the body, and shoots the arrow, or health, into the body. The OHM represents the tremendous height of vibration your music must and will be, to accomplish the deed." (275-11 Reports) For Margret, the letters "MCE" represented words that were associated with her belief that the Christ was instrumental in helping her with healing through her music. In part, the two sets of three columns and five rows are numerical values that Margret felt corresponded to her birth date as a "5" (1-17-1913): $1 + 17 + 1913 = 1 + 8 + 14 = 23 = 5$, and as a "3" (January 17 13): $1 + 1 + 5 + 3 + 1 + 9 + 7 + 1 + 7 + 1 + 3 = 39 = 12 = 3$. According to her notations, the columns are "little tails" that "represent the people who will flock to you to be healed."

The word "OHM" is symbolic of God the Father, the highest influence and vibration as well as her divine ideal. Colors intended for this life seal included the following: both the outer and inner rings, gold (associated with the divine and incorruptibility); the crosses inside the rings, white (purity); the harp, gold; the bow and arrow, gold; the OHM, red (energy and vitality); the strings, red; and the little tails, white.

Gertrude Cayce's Life Seal
Image 4: Painted by Margret Zentgraf

BACKGROUND: Gertrude Cayce was Edgar Cayce's wife and usually conducted the process of her husband giving readings. Both she and Cayce's secretary, Gladys, were instrumental in making Cayce's work possible. She was known for her stability, her love of home and family, and her commitment to the work and spiritual ideals. According to her past-life readings, one of the strongest incarnations having an influence on her in the present was an experience in ancient Egypt in which she had been instrumental in healing and the dissemination of spiritual truths. She was deeply committed to her husband and her two sons, Hugh Lynn and Edgar Evans.

INTERPRETATION OF LIFE SEAL: According to Margret Zentgraf, the seal should be interpreted as follows:

> The rose represents her love that she is shedding out and radiating to her husband and two sons. She being the heart of the big rose and the rest representing her husband. The two small roses represent her two children. The pyramid represents her Egyptian life. (This is about all except that the rose should radiate twelve rays and the pyramid six. Three being her main number besides six and nine.) The rose also represents her love for flowers and the Christ love which she should keep before her, so that everything is done for His love's sake.   538-33 Reports

In addition to the above, "OHM" is symbolic of God, the Father and her divine ideal. The sound of the world can also be representative of her love for the "home." The overarching ribbon suggests that this divine influence overreaches and encompasses all that she does. The rays correspond to an outward radiating influence. The numbers three, six, and nine can be associated with the triune nature of God, beauty/harmony, and wholeness, respectively.

Colors intended for this life seal included the outer ring in gold (associated with the divine and incorruptibility); the overarching ribbon in deep red (energy and vitality); the roses, a lighter red (the color rose is symbolic of love and beauty) and tinted and trimmed with gold; both the pyramid and all the rays were to be in gold, as well.

Gladys Davis' Life Seal
Image 5: Painted by Margret Zentgraf

BACKGROUND: Gladys Davis was Edgar Cayce's secretary and the individual who usually acted as stenographer while Cayce was giving readings. Both she and Cayce's wife, Gertrude, were instrumental in making Cayce's work possible. Deeply committed to the work and to both Mr. and Mrs. Cayce, she had been the daughter born to them in ancient Egypt, according to her past-life readings. In August of 1933, Gladys had expressed feelings of "loneliness and uselessness." In September of that same year, Margret Zentgraf created her life seal in order to help her "overcome her loneliness."

INTERPRETATION OF LIFE SEAL: According to Margret Zentgraf, the seal should be interpreted as follows:

> The star represents the gifts that she has and those that will develop through which she will radiate out help and goodness to many. The pyramid represents her Egyptian Life. Christ represents the ideal that should be ever before her, remembering that Christ went through many sorrows and troubles but through praying to the Father . . . putting everything into His hands, find[ing] true peace, joy and quiet. The angel means that we should have as our goal, perfection, equality with Christ . . . and everyday to better ourselves so that we can come closer to the goal. The OHM should keep the Father ever before her, present in all things . . . The rose represents the sincerity behind everything that she says and does; the purity of thought.

> Thus may this bring her happiness, remembering always
> that our Father in Heaven watches over everyone, even
> you, so that everything that happens will always turn out
> for the best.   288-31 Reports

In addition to the above, the repetition of the number five (e.g., five-pointed star, five rays, and five-sided shape) can be associated with new beginnings, the five senses, resourcefulness and the will (the fifth chakra). The pyramid can also be symbolic of balance and personal transformation.

Colors intended for this life seal included the outer ring in gold (associated with the divine and incorruptibility); blue (associated with spirituality) for the five-sided shape that frames the seal's symbols; both the star and its rays were to be gold; Christ's mantle, blue, His hair golden, and His robe white (purity and perfection); the angel with gold hair, golden wings, and wearing a white robe trimmed in blue; the pyramid and the OHM both colored blue; the rose buds a deep red (the color rose is symbolic of love and beauty; red is symbolic of energy and vitality); and the rose's stem and leaves all in gold.

Life Seal for Mrs. [585]
Image 6: Painted by Virginia Twiford

BACKGROUND: Mrs. [585] was witness to a reading given to another individual before having one herself. Eventually, she would obtain a dozen readings of her own, as well as readings for her husband and her daughter. Deeply involved with the work of Edgar Cayce, she would become a member of the first study group (studying spiritual principles suggested by the readings) and the Glad Helpers (a prayer group devoted to spiritual healing). She would serve as secretary of the prayer group for more than thirty years. According to her readings, influential past-life experiences included incarnations at the time of Jesus, when she had been present and witness to his healing ability, and in ancient Egypt, when she had acted as a counselor and teacher and had been of service to many individuals. Because of longstanding problems with her husband, Mrs. [585] would eventually divorce and go into the field of nursing. While in her eighties, she would write and publish a book on Jesus. She died a week before her eighty-fifth birthday.

INTERPRETATION OF LIFE SEAL: The life seal for Mrs. [585] was described by Edgar Cayce in response to Mrs. [585]'s request for the information:

> (Q) What is my seal?
> (A) Among the seals here we find: *evening* in the distance, the pyramid far away, with the star and crescent rising. We find in the forefront the cinnamon bush, both with its three-pointed leaves and its blossoms and buds. This the symbol of the life for the entity. For, the interpretation is likened unto the symbol; the supplying of life and substance in the foreground to the pyramid in the lessons learned. The star and the crescent, the *Son* of man and His *light* among men!   585-2

In addition to the above, the three-pointed leaves of the cinnamon bush can represent the triune nature of God (as well as the physical, mental, and spiritual nature of humankind). The blossoms and buds are suggestive of this influence springing forth into her life. Keep in mind that when this seal was given, as a member of the first study group she was studying and applying lessons in spiritual growth. The pyramid in the distance is associated with the past-life influence of her Egyptian experience, especially as it relates to healing and the dissemination of spiritual truths. The image of the desert can be suggestive of her Egyptian life, but it might also symbolize the hardship she was having in her personal relationship, as well as her financial challenges.

Life Seal for Miss [1532]
Image 7: Painted by Esther Wynne

BACKGROUND: At the time of her first reading, Miss [1532] was an eighteen-year-old high school graduate. She became interested in the Cayce material through her mother and would have five readings of her own: four physical readings and one life reading. She obtained her life reading in 1938, in part, to help her decide whether to go to business school or college. Her physical readings dealt with such problems as anemia, diet, and poor eliminations and assimilations. During the course of her reading, Edgar Cayce described past lives in Williamsburg, when she had been widowed at a young age, had developed a great deal of independence, and had mastered such things as keeping accounting records and writing letters. Because of these talents, he advised her to go to business school rather than college. When she asked in her reading about the possibility of getting married, Cayce advised her to wait until she was somewhere between twenty-eight and thirty. Another influential past life was given at the time of Jesus, when she had apparently been blessed as a child and had been witness to the miracle of the loaves and the fishes.

Miss [1532] did get married at the age of twenty-nine to an older, divorced man who was a salesman in the office where she worked. The couple had two sons. He died ten years later of cancer, leaving her a young widow.

INTERPRETATION OF LIFE SEAL: The life seal for Miss [1532] was described by Edgar Cayce in response to her request for the information:

(Q) Please give seal and its interpretation.
(A) The seal of the life. A loaf of bread as the center, before which is set the cherubs–and the background rather a sunset with the mountains. Not as of the sacred mountain of China or Japan, but rather that as of Mount Olivet. These are the indications of the interpretations of same: The frugality of the abilities, and yet the supply that is

ever as "Give us this day our daily bread."

This is not, as might be expected, set so that the loaf becomes the most prominent, but as the portion of the whole setting–as to supply the food in spirit, in mind, in body.   1532-1

In addition to the above, the loaf of bread is associated with the staff of life–the source of supply for body, mind, and spirit. It also suggests that regardless of how frugal things may appear to her, she need only call upon the Source of abundant supply. After all, she was personal witness to the miracle of the loaves and fishes and saw the creation of great bounty out of very little. Angels can be symbolic of both a divine presence and a spiritual ideal. A sunset can correspond to personal reflection and introspection. The Mount of Olives is associated with the life and work of Jesus as well as her own incarnation during that period. "Give us this day our daily bread" is from the Lord's Prayer (Matthew 6:9-13), in which Jesus taught the multitudes how to pray.

Life Seal for Mrs. [1770]
Image 8: Painted by Joy Yinger

BACKGROUND: Mrs. [1770] was an enthusiast of the Cayce information, metaphysical studies, and numerology. A widow and former concert singer, she obtained eight readings of her own. In addition to a couple of life readings dealing with the topic of reincarnation, she would have a series of physical readings for sinus problems, anemia, glandular problems, and poor eliminations. For a number of years she maintained a voluminous correspondence with Edgar Cayce about her metaphysical studies, her life, and her travels.

Mrs. [1770] had become the guardian of her niece when the child was six, and she obtained readings for her niece, as well. Her dream was to see her niece married and happy and then move herself to Virginia Beach where she could become more involved with Cayce work. She wrote Mr. Cayce the reason was, "I'll be alone and I want to be useful to someone—somewhere." (1770-8 Reports) She did move to Virginia Beach after her niece's marriage–although it occurred after Edgar Cayce's death–and she became an authority on the subject of numerology. She had a stroke in 1968 from which she recovered and another stroke in 1971, which caused her for a time to be admitted to a nursing home. She recovered again and remained active as a member of her niece's family as well as in A.R.E. She died in 1982 at the age of 93.

INTERPRETATION OF LIFE SEAL: The life seal for Mrs. [1770] was described in one of her life readings:

> (Q) What is my seal?
> (A) That which has been a part, or sought to be a part of, that to represent the order and brotherhood of man; three links that would be joined, upward and downward–the three links set in such a manner, both up and across, as to form a cross. About same would be a wreath entwined with berries, thorns and white blossoms; not as a ribbon, but as a wreath.
>
> This would request not only that which is and has been the experience, but the strength in same to form the greater environs for greater service . . .
>
> Let the seal as indicated be as an emblem–not in the form of something to be worn, but something to be studied each morning or evening when ye would analyze thyself and the motives of others.
>
> Then, as something of drawn work, or as a painting of sufficient size to indicate the union of the links as the three phases of man's experience, as crossed with the three phases of the relationships in the spiritual realm, as crowned by that which represents the purity as well as the blood and the fruit thereof.   1770-3

In terms of the symbolism contained in [1770]'s seal, the interlocking links are suggestive of the interlocking nature of the body, the mind, and the soul and their cooperation and interdependence upon one another. Obviously, the cross is symbolic of spirituality and the Christ and Mrs. [1770]'s connection with Jesus. In fact, one of her life readings confirmed that she had known Jesus in Palestine and had been a follower of His teachings. The wreath of berries, thorns, and flowers that surrounds the interlocking chains takes into account her love for flowers and nature and suggests her appreciation for life's beauty. It can also indicate the energy she puts out to others in all that she does. Finally, as suggested by her reading, the lilies that sit atop her seal are associated with purity, as well as spiritual development, rebirth, and the Christ energy.

Life Seal for Mr. [1467]
Image 9: Painted by Esther Wynne

BACKGROUND: When Mr. [1467] received the reading that mentioned his life seal, he was thirty-three years old. Divorced, he was originally referred to Edgar Cayce by his girlfriend, whom he would later marry. In all, Mr. [1467] obtained a total of nineteen readings for himself on a variety of subjects. The aftereffects of an automobile accident as a child resulted in his requiring physiotherapy treatments and osteopathy, both recommended by the readings. In addition to physical readings, he would also have readings for help with his relationships, a life reading, an aura chart reading, and readings related to business advice. Challenged by several of his relationships in the present, he was encouraged to become a peacemaker.

Employed in the automobile industry, Mr. [1467] was advised that one of his greatest career strengths happened to be in the field of transportation. In part, that ability came from past incarnations, including a past life when he had been one of the sailors (a ship's carpenter) who journeyed to America with Christopher Columbus. In addition to his lifetime as a sailor, another incarnation that was influencing the present was one as a Roman, in which he had become acquainted with the teachings of Jesus through some of His persecuted followers.

After the death of his second wife, he remarried his first wife, saying that their divorce had been his fault and that he was "trying to tie up all the loose ends of karma." He died from a heart attack at the age of sixty-five.

INTERPRETATION OF LIFE SEAL: Mr. [1467]'s life seal was obtained during the course of his third reading:

> (Q) What is my seal?
> (A) A ship (as would be), with the wheel and the cross on same, and the bird of paradise a part of the figure in same. A great deal of color, as may be inferred from the very natures of the figures representing the mien; the wheel as the wheel of life, and as the steering, the guiding influence in the messages or the activities that are represented or illustrated by the ship–carrying the very nature of affiliation or associations with others. Also the bird of paradise represents the peace and harmony that must be kept ever between or in all such associations.   1467-3

The suggestion for "a great deal of color" is indicative of a great deal of emotion, energy, and vitality in everything associated with his life. A bird is often symbolic of a messenger of some kind and the bird of paradise is suggestive of peace and harmony–ingredients he obviously desires to keep in the foreground in his relationships with others. The ship is associated not only with his incarnation as a sailor but also with the concept of a spiritual journey being an influential part of his present experience. Finally, the wheel of life and the cross are symbolic of the central ideal that he desires to have steer and direct his life.

3

Creating Your
Own Life Seal

Perhaps the most important thing to keep in mind when creating a life seal is simply the fact that no artistic ability is required. An individual who wants to make a seal does not need to be an artist or have any experience with drawing, sketching, or painting. She or he does not need to be concerned that the goal is to come up with a finished product or even something that is beautiful. A life seal will not necessarily be seen by anyone else. It is simply a tool for the individual that can be used for personal motivation as well as part of the process of self-discovery.

In creating a life seal, individuals will be attempting to get in touch with something within themselves. The process of drawing, sketching, or painting that seal is simply the act of relating that experience on paper. Although many individuals may wish to draw or paint their life seal, it is just as appropriate to pull together pictures that have been cut from magazines or catalogs. The purpose of creating life seals is not to create a work of beauty. Instead, the purpose is to pull together information from the imagination, from life's experiences, from the unconscious and from an individual's thought processes that might be helpful in calling to mind one's hopes and aspirations regarding the purpose of life. In other words, a life seal can be seen as yet another approach that individuals can use to discover or work with their life's mission.

The Edgar Cayce readings suggest that life seals are essentially "reminders"–reminders of soul strengths, reminders of important experiences, reminders of what the individual hopes to accomplish in the present, and even reminders of shortcomings about which the individual needs to be forewarned. Generally consisting of a few prominent symbols, everything about a personal life seal is intended to call to mind within the individual something about the self. The shapes, the images, the colors, and the design can all be important elements. Regardless of what is contained within a life seal, however, it is usually up to the individual to decide what the symbolism actually means to him or her.

Life seals can be used as a source of personal understanding and guidance. Once a seal has been created, an individual might reflect upon that life seal in the morning and again in the evening as a reminder of her or his individual's purposes, strengths, weaknesses, and direction. By reflecting upon the seal regularly, it can become a tool for evaluating how well the individual is doing as well as an inspirational reminder of one's ultimate desires and goals.

The following information may be helpful in calling to mind experiences, hopes, and dreams and personal reflections about your life–elements that can all be useful in creating a life seal. To begin, you might wish to pull together the "Materials needed to create your life seal." Afterwards, you may wish to review the following lists: "Things that can be helpful to remember in creating your life seals" and "Possible methods of obtaining symbols for life seals." There is also a life seal reverie, "A Journey into Your Imagination," that may be helpful in gathering symbols and images for the creation of your personal life seal.

Materials needed to create your life seal:
- White cardboard or heavy-weight white paper
- Generally, a circle drawn on the cardboard of approximately eight to fourteen inches in diameter
- Colored pencils, crayons, paints, or watercolors (or a variety of magazines that you can use to cut out appropriate pictures and then glue them onto your life seal)

Things that can be helpful to remember in creating your life seal:
(In other words, what kinds of pictures, symbols, colors, images, or even words will be helpful to you in calling to mind some of these things?)
- Things you would like to have more of
- Things that you are good at
- Things that you enjoy doing
- Things that are challenging for you
- Things you need to work on
- Things that are a part of your life's purpose
- Things that will make your life more balanced

Possible methods of obtaining symbols for life seals:
- Using guided imagery (see Life Seal Relaxation and Reverie)
- Trying meditation and relaxation
- Calling to mind reoccurring dream images and symbols
- Listening to inspirational music
- Thinking of your own aspirations, hopes, and ideals
- Working with inspirational writing
- Working with movement or dance
- Calling to mind your talents and abilities
- Thinking of your favorite colors
- Recalling places or images that remind you of special memories from your life
- Working with your own intuition or getting a psychic reading
- Listing symbols that remind you of your favorite hobbies
- Listing historical eras or cultures that you feel drawn to

- Reading from scriptures or uplifting verse
- Contemplating whether your body's markings—moles, birthmarks, etc.—can tell you something about yourself
- Taking time for introspection and self-analysis (e.g., considering such things as what you need to develop in yourself, what you need to change, etc.)
- Considering what other people have described as your personal strengths and weaknesses
- Reflecting upon what you have daydreamed about becoming
- Remembering any designs/shapes that you seem drawn to
- Considering whether you habitually make any persistent doodles
- Pondering the astrological (and/or numerological) influences that are most influential in your life
- Pondering any repeating patterns or experiences that have been a part of your life
- Listing your favorite activities or things you enjoy being a part of (e.g., nature, animals, hobbies, swimming, horses, sports, etc.)
- Contemplating your purpose or mission in life

A JOURNEY INTO YOUR IMAGINATION: LIFE SEAL RELAXATION AND REVERIE

Note: A reverie is best done with another person (reading the reverie like a script), or with oneself first narrating the reverie on a tape and then playing it back in order to experience the exercise. Reveries are generally narrated at about one-third the normal rate of speech.

NARRATION:

Life Seal Reverie:
   Get comfortable in your chair (or lying down) and close your eyes. Take a deep breath and tell yourself to relax. Take another deep breath—breathing in relaxation and calm and slowly breathing out any tension or stress. If there is some part of your body that needs to relax, tense up the muscles in that area and hold it; hold it and then relax. Then relax some more. Take another deep breath and relax.

As you become more comfortable and relaxed, focus your attention on your breathing. Let your awareness begin to notice how the air feels cool as you inhale and how it feels warm as you breathe out. Continue to breathe and relax. Breathe in this cool sense of relaxation all through your body. Remain comfortable and very much at peace. Listen to the sound of my voice and relax. Breathe in relaxation. Breathe out tension. Just spend a few moments in this peaceful state of relaxation. [Pause.]

Now in your imagination, I want you to think back to a positive memory from your childhood. What is one of your most enjoyable memories from your childhood? Remember a time from your childhood when you were experiencing joy or happiness. [Pause.] Where are you? Who are you with? What are you doing? What are some of the things you enjoyed doing as a child? As a child, can you remember some of the things you wanted to be when you grew up?

Next in your imagination, I want you to think about some of the positive things people may have said about you throughout your life. What have people said about your qualities, your talents, your traits? What are some of the qualities people may have repeatedly noticed about you throughout your life? Have individuals mentioned such things as being creative? Being a good listener? Being an optimist? What are some of the positive qualities or strengths that others have noticed or perhaps you have noticed about yourself? Whatever it may be, think about one or more of the talents or strengths you possess within yourself. Is there a symbol or image that could symbolize any of these talents or abilities? [Pause.]

After you think about your strengths, can you think about areas in your life where you may need to work on aspects of yourself? In other words, have you noticed any recurring weaknesses that you would like to change within yourself? For example, are you impatient? Do you need to work on your own self-esteem? Are you short-tempered? Do you have a tendency to put things off until the last minute? Whatever it may be, think about something that you would like to change or develop within yourself. Is there a symbol that can remind you of something that you need to work on? [Pause.]

Next in your imagination, think about a period in history or a culture that you have always felt drawn to. In other words, is there a time period in the history of the world that really appeals to you? Another way of thinking of this is to ask yourself, "If I could spend a day with any figure from history, who might it be?" [Pause.] Is there a place in the world that you have always wanted to visit?

In your imagination, think about some of the things that you like to do in the present. For example, are there hobbies that you are drawn to? If you could do anything with your free time, what would that be? If you could be anywhere right now doing your favorite thing with some of your favorite people, where would you be and what would you be doing? If you could be doing anything with your life right now, what would that entail? [Pause.]

Next, I want you to think about any colors or patterns that you are most drawn to. In other words, what colors of clothing are most prominent in your closet? What colors of furniture or carpeting or paint is most prominent throughout your home? What color or colors would you describe as your favorite? [Pause.]

Now in your imagination, think about one of the most memorable *positive* people from your life. Is there a person that you really admired (or admire) and want to be more like? Think about one of the most positive people who have influenced your life. See that individual standing before you and feel what it feels like to be in this individual's presence. [Pause.] What is one of the most outstanding qualities that you associate with that person? If you could be more like this individual in some manner, how might that feel? [Pause.]

Conversely, there have probably been people in your life that have been frustrating or challenging. Think about one of the most challenging individuals that has ever crossed your life's path. See that individual standing before you and feel what it feels like to be in this person's presence. [Pause.] Is there an irritating behavior or trait that you see evident in this person that might also be a part of your self? If you could change one frustrating thing about your self, how might that feel? How might that influence your relationships with others? [Pause.]

Next in your imagination, I want you to ask yourself, "What is the purpose of my life?" and then listen. See if your imagination can tell you what one of the main purposes of your lifetime right now is all about. Ask, "What is the purpose of my life?" [Pause.] If you could be doing this purpose right now, how might you spend the course of each day? [Pause.] Is there a symbol, a picture, or an image that will remind you of that purpose?

Finally, in your imagination, I want you to imagine yourself sitting in your chair (or lying down). See yourself breathing in relaxation. See yourself firmly grounded in the present. See yourself collecting together all of the images and pictures that have been a part of this imagination exercise. Take one more breath, imagining yourself in this time, in this place, right now and open your eyes.

Note: You may wish to begin working on your life seal while these images and memories are still fresh in your mind.

CREATING YOUR OWN LIFE SEAL

After reflecting upon the above questions, ideas, and images, decide upon approximately three to eight pictures, images, or symbols that will call to mind the most important things that you would like to remember each day about your life and your life's direction at this time. For example, if "family" was an important image for you, you may wish to draw a house in your life seal or literally include a picture of your family within the borders of your seal. If one of your soul talents that you wish to express more fully is music, then you might wish to include the picture of a musical instrument, such as a harp. Imagine that the emotional quality you want to express more fully is love, then an appropriate symbol for your life seal could be a heart. If one of the things you want to change about yourself is overcoming a short temper or being quick to anger, then you might decide to incorporate the color red (which can be associated with anger or aggression) as a reminder of something you need to look out for during the course of a day. On the other hand, you might simply decide to write the word "anger" with an "X" through it as a reminder of the same thing. If you have always felt drawn to the period of initiation and ceremony associated with ancient Egypt, then a picture of the Great

Pyramid or the Sphinx could be appropriate for your personal seal. However you decide to create your life seal, have a good time, make it fun, and don't worry about the artistic quality because this is something you are creating just for you.

Possible Creation of Personal Life Seal

The Edgar Cayce readings suggest that life seals can be used as reminders. Each morning upon awakening you might want to look at your seal as a reminder of what you hope to accomplish during the course of the day, what you hope to work on, and what talents or traits you hope to cultivate or change within yourself. Before going to sleep at night, you might decide to look at your seal once more as a means of reflecting upon the day's successes as well as those experiences and interactions that might not have measured up to the best that you hope to accomplish in the future. A life seal is really a personal symbol that can awaken within you the desire to know who you really are, the consciousness of what you ultimately hope to become and an awareness of your ongoing relationship with the divine.

Life seals can be changed, revised, or redrawn whenever you feel the need to remotivate yourself or reemphasize some other quality or aspiration. From this perspective, a life seal can be viewed as a roadmap for your personal direction from the moment it is created. Once elements of that direction are achieved (or their desired outcome has changed), it is appropriate to take the time to create a new life seal that more fully represents where you are at any moment in time. To be sure, such things as your ultimate life's purpose or your highest aspirations and dreams may not change, but certain qualities you wish to develop within yourself or behavior you wish to transform might vary with time.

Using life seals is one of the tools for working with personal symbolism that was frequently recommended by the Edgar Cayce readings. A life seal is simply a drawing or artistic rendering of symbols, pictures, and images that can assist you in better understanding who you really are while reminding you of what you ultimately hope to become. Creating and then working with a life seal can be helpful for any individual interested in personal growth and transformation, spiritual development, self-awareness, or focusing upon her or his life's direction.

Image 1
Edgar Cayce's Life Seal, painted by Miss [2486]

Image 2
Edgar Cayce's Life Seal, painted by Margret Zentgraf

Image 3
Margret Zentgraf's Personal Life Seal, drawn by herself

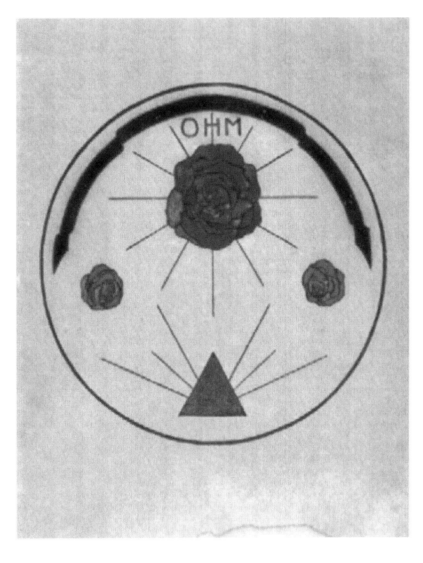

Image 4
Gertrude Cayce's Life Seal, painted by Margret Zentgraf

Image 5
Gladys Davis' Life Seal, painted by Margret Zentgraf

Image 6
Life Seal for Mrs. [585], painted by Virginia Twiford

Image 7
Life Seal for Miss [1532], painted by Esther Wynne

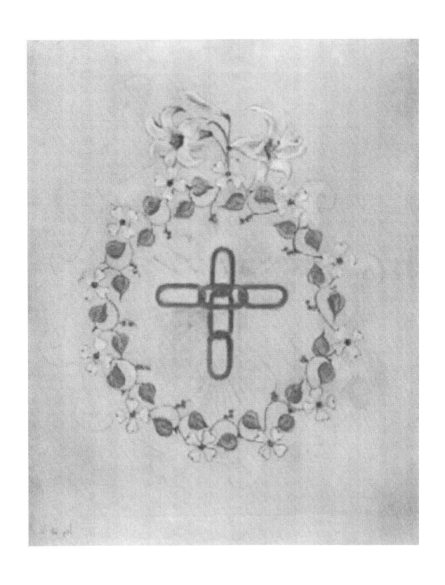

Image 8
Life Seal for Mrs. [1770], painted by Joy Yinger

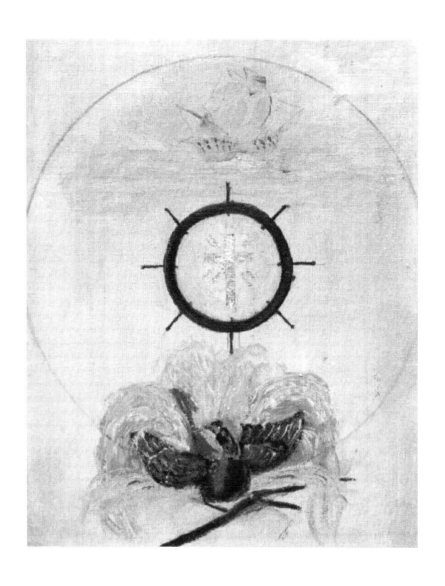

Image 9
Life Seal for Mr. [1467], painted by Esther Wynne

Part Two: Aura Charts

It would be very sad, were I to relate all the misery and privations which the poor little duckling endured during the hard winter; but when it had passed, he found himself lying one morning in a moor, amongst the rushes. He felt the warm sun shining, and heard the lark singing, and saw that all around was beautiful spring. Then the young bird felt that his wings were strong, as he flapped them against his sides, and rose high into the air. They bore him onwards, until he found himself in a large garden, before he well knew how it had happened. The apple-trees were in full blossom, and the fragrant elders bent their long green branches down to the stream which wound round a smooth lawn. Everything looked beautiful, in the freshness of early spring. From a thicket close by came three beautiful white swans, rustling their feathers, and swimming lightly over the smooth water. The duckling remembered the lovely birds, and felt more strangely unhappy than ever.

Excerpt from *The Ugly Duckling*
Hans Christian Andersen, 1844

4

The Aura Chart as a Map of the Soul's Journey

Perhaps one of the most interesting and at the same time overlooked tools for exploring personal symbolism in the Edgar Cayce readings is the information on the subject of aura charts. In appearance an aura chart is simply an oblong document much like a tapestry or an open scroll that utilizes symbols and pictures to record both the highlights and the low points of a soul's journey through various lifetimes. Drawing upon the major incarnations having an influence on an individual in the present, an aura chart is essentially a physical manifestation of a portion of the Akashic Records—the universal record of the soul's journey. Used in a manner similar to life seals, the readings suggest that the symbols and images used in aura charts can bring to the mind of an individual an awareness of her or his soul's strengths, purposes, and innate weaknesses. The chart portrays a soul's successes and shortcomings—what has been learned as well as where a soul has erred in its journey through history.

The background for aura charts can be traced to two people and their respective psychic talents: Edgar Cayce and his lifelong ability to see auras and an artist from New York named Nancy Lansdale, who had the ability to perceive energy patterns above individuals. For Edgar Cayce, each individual appeared to have an aura–a series of vibrating colors that seemed to surround an individual and provide a barometer of that person's health, state of mind, strengths, weaknesses, desires, thoughts, and more. In the 1940s, Cayce described his experience with auras, as follows:

> Ever since I can remember I have seen colors in connection with people. I do not remember a time when the human beings I encountered did not register on my retina with blues and greens and reds gently pouring from their heads and shoulders. It was a long time before I realized that other people did not see these colors; it was a long time before I heard the word aura, and learned to apply it to this phenomenon which to me was commonplace. I do not ever think of people except in connection with their auras; I see them change in my friends and loved ones as time goes by—sickness, dejection, love, fulfillment— these are all reflected in the aura, and for me the aura is the weathervane of the soul. It shows which way the winds of destiny are blowing. (Cayce, *Auras*, pg. 5)

In the case of Nancy Lansdale, Nancy claimed that the energy pattern she saw for each individual was so distinct that she could even see it from a photograph. Eventually, she decided to use her artistic talent to draw these energy patterns in colored pastel chalk, depicting for others what she was seeing. She called these depictions "archetypal drawings." In 1946, psychologist Gina Cerminara described Nancy's ability to see energy patterns:

> . . . Nancy Lansdale of New York City . . . some twenty years ago . . . discovered that she had the strange faculty

of seeing light symbols above people's heads. She had for some time previous seen the aura; but this was different from the aura: it hung like a chandelier above the head and the light which emanated from it merged with the aura but was distinct from it. Unlike the aura, the pattern of symbols remained constant from birth to death; moreover it was as distinct and individual for each person as his face or fingerprint. And so, after much study and observation, Mrs. Lansdale interpreted this strange and beautiful thing to be the individual's energy pattern, upon which the structure of his body and personality was based. (Cerminara, "Archetypes and Aura Charts," pg. 1)

Due to her enthusiasm for Edgar Cayce's work, in 1941 Nancy created an archetypal drawing for Cayce, depicting her perception of his energy pattern. Because of the drawing, Edgar Cayce would pursue the subject of aura charts in thirty-one readings given over a seventeen-month period (August 1941 to January 1943) during World War II.

Archetypal Drawing for Edgar Cayce
Image 10: Drawn by Nancy Lansdale—at the end of Chapter Six.

In order to understand more fully his archetypal drawing, on August 24, 1941, Edgar Cayce obtained a reading asking for an interpretation of Nancy's artwork. The reading said that the drawing was essentially the artist's attempt to express her perception of the aura and the vibrations surrounding Edgar Cayce. The reading went on to interpret some of the symbolism, such as the stars representing the energy of activity as well as ideals. The irregular figures could be said to correspond to ideas. The tiny J-like image in the bottom foreground of the drawing was a tadpole, representing "the beginning." The repeated use of three symbols of the same thing corresponded to body, mind, and soul. The various depictions of a cross, corresponded to Cayce's being centered in the cross. In fact, the reading added that in spite of Cayce's various shortcomings this commitment "may be said to be the saving grace in this individual entity." The reading repeatedly cautioned, however, that Nancy Lansdale's perception of Cayce's balance—as depicted by the layout, symmetry, and uniformity of the drawing—was not as factual as the artist would suppose:

> . . . do not understand that the activity of the individual entity [Edgar Cayce] has been or is as symmetrical as expressed here. It is rather the beauty of same that is expressed by the artist than the individual entity; for the entity has not been very much of the artist in patterning his life to those things even expressed . . .
>
> As is indicated in this particular archetype, there is a unison . . . indicating an individual entity very well balanced—from the artist's standpoint, at least; though do not think that this is so in the individual entity! It is as the artist views it!   294-204

Because of the interest stimulated by Nancy's drawing and the subsequent reading, two weeks later Edgar Cayce's secretary, Gladys Davis, requested her own reading. Gladys hoped to see whether or not the readings could describe a "complete spiritual aura" that could be drawn and utilized as a helpful influence in her life. While in the trance state, Cayce told her that what she really wanted was "an aura chart" and he proceeded to describe a drawing that would trace her soul's spiritual development from the dawn of time up to the present through a series of pictures and symbols.

Beginning with the reading given to Gladys Davis and then for all those that would follow, the aura chart readings systematically describe the creation of each chart beginning with the bottom and proceeding to the top. The bottom of the chart depicts the earliest incarnation having an influence on the individual in the present. After that, each level of the chart illustrates the next subsequent lifetime and historical period having a major influence on the present. Toward the top of the chart can be found the most recent incarnation bearing upon the present as well as the highest spiritual ideal or attainment toward which the individual is striving.

Rich in symbolism, each level of an aura chart corresponding to various lifetimes also depicts the mental influences and the level of consciousness that affected the individual in that particular life. In Cayce's detailed descriptions of the chart, planetary symbols (including the sun and the moon) often represent specific attainments or lessons learned and the twelve signs of the zodiac frequently surround the planetary symbols and correspond to the consciousness or level of awareness that accompanied those lessons. Generally, on the left is drawn the consciousness, hope, or talents with which the individual entered a specific lifetime, whereas on the right is pictured the attainment and level of consciousness actually achieved by the individual during that same period. For some individuals the chart is filled with easy-to-understand pictures that obviously correspond to specific historical epochs; however, for others, the chart consists mostly of a series of signs and symbols that are perhaps best understood by the individual. In describing the charts, Cayce apparently chose those symbols that would best resonate to the individual for whom the chart was being created.

In 1942, Edgar Cayce described the readings' involvement with aura charts in a letter to one of his supporters:

> The life readings are attracting more attention than usual these days, and most all say they get the greatest good from them, and I believe most do who study their own readings.
>
> The aura chart reading is another fancy idea seemingly hatched up in the readings, but the charts are very beautiful when they are worked out and painted according to the suggestions. Many say they are the real daily checks on the body . . . they are certainly an interesting daily reminder if they are hung where they can be seen.   779-19 Reports

The readings suggested that each aura chart was to somehow encapsulate the individuality of the person for whom it was created. It would help to create an awareness of an individual's activities, intents, experiences, and relationships to others. The readings also described why having a physical depiction of the chart might be helpful, as in the case of a thirty-year-old housewife who had requested an aura chart reading of her own:

> Yet, as a drawing, this should constantly bring to the entity's mind the activities, or manners of activity, indicating the thought and the purpose which has been a part of the entity's experience; thus enabling the entity to visualize why this, that or the other appeals to the entity, why this, that or the other may be a shortcoming, or why certain things appeal and others do not.   2175-5

Eventually, Edgar Cayce obtained an aura chart reading for himself, and Esther Wynne, head of the A.R.E. Study Group work, painted it for him.

Aura Chart for Edgar Cayce
Image 11: Painted by Esther Wynne

The aura chart painted for Edgar Cayce depicts a series of the six lifetimes most influencing him when the reading for the chart was given. Obviously, these are not the only incarnations Cayce attributed to himself. Instead, these are the lifetimes most affecting him at the time of the reading. These same six lifetimes had also been repeatedly discussed in various life readings obtained by Edgar Cayce over the years. Beginning at the bottom of the painting and moving toward the top, the six illustrations correspond to the following periods in history: (1) Creation; (2) Atlantis; (3) ancient Egypt; (4) ancient Persia; (5) Palestine; and, (6) eighteenth-century America. As a means of more fully understanding the chart, additional historical and biographical information, and the corresponding illustrations suggested in Edgar Cayce's aura chart reading (294-206), an explanation of the symbolism is as follows:

THE CREATION PERIOD ILLUSTRATION:
Cayce's aura chart reading stated that the bottom of his chart should

depict the period when souls first incarnated into the material plane, "when the morning stars sang together and the sons of God came together announcing the advent of man[kind] into material consciousness." The reading suggested that the picture needed to illustrate a brand new world, with a rising sun, animals, and lush vegetation. Precise in detail, the animals that were suggested for the picture included a snake in one of the trees, ravens, doves, an ox, and a camel. Without exception, all of the animals were to be staring toward the rising sun with a look of "expectancy."

On the right-hand side of the illustration, Cayce suggested drawing a crescent moon surrounded by seven five-pointed stars. In part, this represents the emotions (the moon) coming together with the five senses (the number five) and the spiritual forces (the number seven), all in a state of primordial paradise.

The planetary symbols prescribed for this period were the sun on the left, indicating the entrance of the Creative Force into the material plane, and the earth on the right, suggesting the attainment of third-dimensional consciousness.

THE ATLANTIS ILLUSTRATION:

The Cayce readings suggest that during a portion of the Atlantis period there was a time when souls had not yet separated into the male and female sexes but instead incarnated as the two sexes in one. The Atlantean period was also a time when some souls still retained their remembrance of their connection to the divine whereas others had become encased in materiality, forgetting their spiritual origins. During this time there were also half-human "things"—humanoidal creatures that were being used as slaves by those who felt themselves superior to others.

The illustration shows some figures staring toward the light and others held in chains of bondage. For some the chains symbolize servitude and slavery; for others the chains are a symbol of being unable to catch a vision of the light. In the center of the illustration there is also depicted a mountain and the Atlantean crystal off in the distance—the source of the continent's power. The reading advised placing the symbol for Gemini (suggesting the two sexes in one) near the mountain.

During this period, the soul that would become Edgar Cayce had been involved in bringing spiritual teachings to the people, uplifting many in the process. At the same time, however, according to the readings, he and his soul partner had apparently been overcome with the desires of the flesh (288-6).

The planetary symbol prescribed for this period was the symbol for Mercury on the left, surrounded by four symbols of Aries. This could indicate coming into the earth (the number four can correspond to the material plane) with wisdom (Mercury) and leadership abilities (Aries). On the right, the reading advised the placement of Jupiter surrounded by four symbols of Scorpio. This would suggest having broad vision and universality of thinking (Jupiter); however, it could also indicate acquiring sexual excess during this period (Scorpio).

THE ANCIENT EGYPTIAN ILLUSTRATION:

According to Edgar Cayce's own life readings, one of the periods when his soul had made the greatest advancement had been during an ancient Egyptian incarnation as a high priest named Ra Ta. The illustration shows a leader (with staff in hand) being followed by a group of people. The reading suggested that a few "beasts of burden" be depicted in the drawing, such as a donkey, a camel, and an elephant, since this lifetime included a period of exile in the Nubian desert. It was also recommended that a pyramid under construction be shown in the center of the drawing, indicating that this was during the time when the Great Pyramid was being built. On the right of the drawing was to be shown two Egyptian temples (the Temple Beautiful and the Temple of Sacrifice), which had been used for such things as rituals, healing, and personal development. The readings even recommended that two lights be drawn coming from the entrance to the temples: a white light, suggesting the spirit and the Creative Forces, and a green light, suggestive of the energy of healing.

Rather than astrological symbols being associated with this particular lifetime, the readings indicated the placement of a heart on the left, suggesting coming into the earth with divine love, and a cross on the right, suggesting the attainment of mastery over the physical plane.

THE ANCIENT PERSIA ILLUSTRATION:

The fourth lifetime depicted in Edgar Cayce's aura chart is an incarnation in ancient Persia, when he had been a desert leader in a "city in the hills and plains" by the name of Uhjltd (pronounced "Yoolt"). During that period, Cayce had been mortally wounded. Rather than dying, however, somehow he had been able to detach himself from his physical body. During this out-of-body experience he healed himself and went on to become a prominent healer and leader. In his lifetime as Edgar Cayce, his ability to detach himself from physical consciousness and tune in to intuitive information was traced to this incarnation.

The drawing depicts a lame figure upon a series of rock terraces. On one of the ledges of the rocks is a raven, suggesting the possibility of death. On another ledge are two doves. The dove can suggest the possibility of divine information or spirit coming into the earth; the number two can also be a symbol for companionship. According to Cayce's readings, during this period Uhjltd came together again with the individual with whom he had been connected in Atlantis—apparently the two overcoming their earlier excesses during this experience.

One planetary symbol prescribed for this period was the symbol for Venus on the left, surrounded by four of the zodiac signs for Pisces, suggesting love and beauty (Venus) being influenced by spirituality and intuition (Pisces). On the right, the reading indicated that the symbol for Uranus was to be drawn, surrounded by four Libras. Uranus can be associated with psychic insight as well as one who is prone to going to extremes. Libra often corresponds to balance or idealism.

THE PALESTINE ILLUSTRATION:

According to the readings, at this period in Edgar Cayce's soul history he had an incarnation in Palestine when he had been known as Lucius of Cyrene. Originally a soldier of fortune for the Romans, Lucius had been so influenced by the life of Jesus that he had eventually become one of the leaders of the early Church. He had also learned humility and to be "anchored in the cross" during that lifetime.

The illustration was detailed as having three people in a boat with a very small mast. They were described as being a middle-aged man

[Lucius?], a younger man, and a girl, all clothed in Eastern attire. In order to suggest being anchored in the cross, on the right side of the boat was to be an anchor and on the left a golden cross.

The readings advised placing the planetary symbol for Mercury on the left, surrounded by Leo. This could indicate an individual who possesses a great deal of wisdom (Mercury) and organizational abilities (Leo). On the right Mars symbolized those qualities attained during this incarnation, surrounded by Aries. This might suggest the energies of personal action (Mars) being channeled into leadership abilities (Aries).

THE EIGHTEENTH-CENTURY AMERICA ILLUSTRATION:

The final scene is a picture of the lifetime when Edgar Cayce had lived as an early American scout, womanizer, and drifter by the name of John Bainbridge. Of English descent, Bainbridge had eventually traveled west and become a regular in the Fort Dearborn area (present-day Chicago). There he was known to lead astray the affections and morals of many women. He would later lose his life on a river raft in the midst of escaping a battle. In spite of possessing many talents and abilities as a soul, Cayce, himself, later described this lifetime as a period in which he had been an individual who was "a ne'er-do-well, one of those people who didn't do anything but make a lot of trouble." (464-32 Reports)

The central picture is supposed to be the illustration of a bar and brothel, with a dancing girl entertaining the crowd. On the right is a small sailboat, the kind that Bainbridge himself might have used for scouting along the riverbanks. On the left is the river and raft upon which the individual eventually lost his life.

In terms of astrological symbols depicting consciousness attained and lessons learned, on the left is the symbol for Neptune surrounded by Gemini. The symbols suggest that the soul entered with a great capacity for mysticism and clairvoyance (Neptune) as well as strong mental abilities and communication skills (Gemini). However, Gemini can also indicate an individual who is prone to restlessness.

The symbols on the right are the earth surrounded by Libra. This might suggest that the individual was overcome by the material and physical world (earth) but somehow realized at a soul level the need to learn balance (Libra).

POSSIBLE ATTAINMENTS ILLUSTRATION:

The final symbols suggested for Edgar Cayce's aura chart included a golden eight-pointed star, the all-seeing eye and a cross. The star can be a symbol for the ideal. The number eight can be associated with attainment or balance. The all-seeing eye can correspond to singleness of vision. Gold is the color for spiritual truths, possible attainments and that which is invaluable. Finally, the cross is often representative of the Christ, spirituality, and mastery over the physical plane.

Taken together, Edgar Cayce's aura chart shows an overall depiction of his soul's strengths and weaknesses, the periods in history that were bearing the greatest degree of influence upon him at the time, his highest hopes and aspirations, and the innate shortcomings about which he could best be forewarned.

In addition to painting Edgar Cayce's aura chart, Esther Wynne made a study of the aura chart readings for years and actually painted the greatest number of charts still contained in the Edgar Cayce archives. Around 1956, Esther discussed her understanding of these charts, as follows:

> The aura chart is taken from the Book of Life of the individual. It is a symbol of life and not just a picture nor a group of pictures. Yet pictures and symbols are used because they convey more than words. They indicate the manner in which a particular phase of the experience was manifested and various stages of development in sojourns in the earth.
>
> They not only recall experiences, but relieve stress— show individuals how they may draw upon past experiences. They not only show the beautiful in life, but the sordid, the gladness in suffering; the successes, the failures, the strength, the hopes. But most of all the aura chart gives the attainments that may be reached and how we may realize our relationship to the universe.

> The signs on the right of the aura charts usually indicate that which or in which the entity enters [she means left as suggested by reading 2533-5]; that with the hope of the activity is directed. The sign upon the left [she means right] indicates the attainments, if any. The signs around the planets show the manner of activity.
>
> These symbols–from astrological influences–do not surpass the will but are only used to indicate developments made and aspirations that may be attained for the individual.
>
> Aura charts are based on reincarnation, and are meaningless to those who do not believe in it. 5746-1 Reports

Years later, artist, psychic, and author Ingo Swann would call the descriptions given in the Edgar Cayce readings for the creation of aura charts "the nucleus of a transpersonal art form." (Swann, pg. 1) For that reason the process of working with (and even creating) an aura chart may provide an impetus for self-understanding, personal growth, and an awareness of one's interactions with others. As Cayce suggests, the aura chart is a map of the soul's journey/experiences/lessons/needs and can provide an individual with greater self-awareness and may even create a motivation to cultivate soul strengths while overcoming innate weaknesses.

Using the 126 symbols and images detailed in the readings, as well as the colors and positions associated with them, Ingo Swann painted the Edgar Cayce aura chart following the guideline suggested in Cayce's own reading: " . . . much depends upon the concept of the artist in making such a drawing a thing of beauty, or a helpful experience for an entity." (294-206)

The Edgar Cayce Aura Chart
Image 12: Painted by Ingo Swann

In July 1942, Esther Wynne requested a reading in which she asked a series of questions regarding the creation of aura charts. During the course of that reading, Cayce described the difference between aura charts and life seals. He said, in part:

> . . . while a plaque [life seal] is usually as the reminder of some individual fact or act to be attained or discarded, and it is indicated in the information given respecting such. On the other hand, the aura chart—to those who would study same (for little comes of itself)—is for the individual until it has fully attained. Who has attained?
>
> 5746-1

When Esther wondered about what size to make the aura chart painting, the readings advice was that it was simply a matter of personal choice: "Whether you make the paper two inches wide or two feet wide or four feet, that is to be the choice of the artist!"

While discussing the topic of aura charts, Cayce also provided the general interpretation of a number of colors and symbols that were frequently used within the charts. For example, the color white was said to often correspond to purity. Gold could be associated with personal attainment. Dark blue might indicate an awakening. Purple might represent spiritual healing. Violet could symbolize the act of seeking. Coral was often associated with material mindedness. Gray could correspond with moodiness. In terms of symbols, one meaning associated with the moon was change. On occasion, the sun could represent strength or life. A seven-pointed star could correspond to attainments within the seven centers of the body, whereas a five-pointed star might indicate an attainment through personal activity. (For an examination and interpretation of over 300 symbols refer to the Appendix.)

As already mentioned, numbers also play an important role in the depiction of aura charts. Although there can be multiple meanings for each number, numeral one can correspond to the beginning. Two can be associated with duality or companionship. Three is often a symbol for the triune nature of God or the body-mind-spirit. The number four can represent the material plane. The readings often use five to symbolize the five senses. Six might indicate beauty and harmony. The use of seven can indicate spirituality or it might correspond to the seven spiritual centers or chakras. The number eight can be associated with attainment or balance. Nine can sometimes represent wholeness, etc.

Charts for a number of people contain similar symbols that were to be depicted within each individual's drawing. For example, several individuals were told that their soul had apparently experienced a period of questioning in one or more incarnations. That period might have been a time of personal reflection or it could have been one of calling to mind the rationale behind certain actions. In order to best illustrate that time in the soul's journey, Cayce suggested that a question mark be included in the depiction of the chart (379-18, 1226-3, and 1467-12).

A number of individuals were told that the drawing of a cornucopia or a horn of plenty needed to be included within their respective charts as a means illustrating the act of pouring forth such things as the fruits of the spirit (303-31, 1223-5, 2390-6, and others). These fruits of the spirit could be depicted as fruit, on other occasions they might be drawn as diamonds or they could even be written out as the literal words of "faith," "hope," "love," "patience," and so forth.

The picture of a rainbow was sometimes suggested as a way of symbolizing the seven spiritual centers, hope, awakening consciousness, or even ultimate personal attainment (2175-5, 2378-2, 2753-1, and others). The seven spiritual centers could also be symbolized as a seven-pointed candelabrum or as seven candles (404-11 and 538-72).

Many of the aura charts include an all-seeing eye and/or a cross to represent such things as ideals, an awareness of the divine, or the presence of God (294-206, 1709-9, 2648-2, and others). In a similar manner, the drawing of a dove or doves was often used to illustrate the presence of the divine or the act of spirit coming into the earth (263-17, 1467-12, and others).

It was not uncommon for some of the charts to include words or phrases that could bring to mind something important to the individual. For example, some of the charts contain the letter "G," which was to represent God, Jehovah, or the presence of the divine. On other occasions the word or name "EL" was suggested to mean the same thing (379-18, 2072-7, 2651-1, and others), perhaps corresponding to

Elohim (God) or El Shaddai (God Almighty).

As a final example, a number of the charts contain an open book or the Holy Bible, indicating a personal spiritual search or the attainment of spiritual truths (357-14, 585-10, 1523-14, and others).

Certainly, each chart also contains individual symbols that are not necessarily depicted in any other aura chart, as in the case of a scarab (an Egyptian beetle) symbolizing "attainments" (1223-5), a schooner with three masts corresponding to a Norse incarnation (404-11), or an hourglass representing the passage of time (2648-2).

As already pointed out in Edgar Cayce's aura chart, all of the charts generally contain specific references to planetary symbols and zodiacal signs that correspond to each of the incarnations being illustrated. For example, a thirty-two-year-old woman had been told of a lifetime in Atlantis in which she had been a student of the Law of One, a proponent of equality and an individual who had truly learned to be of love and service. She was advised to put the symbol of the moon surrounded by the sign of Cancer to the right of the picture that illustrated her Atlantean incarnation:

> Upon the right side of the chart, on the level with the base of the stone [the Tuaoi stone, which can symbolize the power of Atlantis], put again the full moon; the face here the more representative in the pink or red. The figures about this, four in number, would be represented in the sign Cancer.   2072-7

In part, the moon could symbolize feminine qualities such as emotions, feelings, and intuition. The color pink or red can correspond to love. The number four often represents the material plane. The influence of Cancer can be associated with emotions, sensitivity, and a love of the home. Taken together, this image would suggest that the individual had truly been able to manifest empathy and a feeling for others in that incarnation. The depth of symbolism utilized by the Edgar Cayce readings is truly impressive, for this level of detail is provided for each of the five or six lifetimes (both coming into the earth and departing from it), given for each individual on every single aura chart.

At the same time, the readings suggest that any one lifetime contained in a chart is not necessarily to be stressed above any other—apparently, a soul's high and low points are both to be pondered equally.

In addition to a variety of symbols and astrological influences that some of the charts share in common, many of the individual aura charts contain illustrations that correspond to the same periods in history given for other individuals. In other words, because aura charts provide a map of the soul's journey and because many of Cayce's contemporaries had been associated with one another in the past, it was not unusual for identical historical periods to show up in individual aura charts. However, drawings used to illustrate those same historical periods were often tailored specifically to the individual.

For example, the period of Creation might be symbolized as a picture illustrating "when the morning stars sang together and the sons of God came together announcing the advent of man[kind] into material consciousness" (294-206) or as a lotus flower blooming atop a mucky pool of water, suggesting the birth of an individual soul from out of the substance of a primordial universe (2390-6).

A lifetime in Atlantis could be symbolized by a map of the continent, which Cayce said resembled Australia (303-31); a field growing with corn, wheat, and barley, which the reading identified as the activity of the individual in that lifetime (2301-3); or, as the Atlantean crystal or Tuaoi stone (2072-7).

Ancient Egypt was often depicted with the pyramids or the Sphinx (1152-14, 1709-9, 2533-5, and others). However, for an individual who had served the Egyptian ruler as a diplomat during a time of chaos, the suggested illustration was a picture of an emissary negotiating with the ruler and a layman (415-9). On another occasion, an individual was told that his experiences in ancient Egypt might best be represented with a drawing of a wheel with four spokes, a papyrus branch and an apple tree (533-20). A fourth person was informed that during her Egyptian experience she had truly excelled in motherhood and her love for children. With that in mind, it was suggested that her aura chart include a picture of the goddess Isis with Horus upon her lap to indicate that experience (538-72).

An incarnation during the period of the Roman Empire was illustrated for one person as two men carrying the banner of Rome, one with a shield and the other with an ax (845-8). For another individual, that same historical period was shown with a picture of a Roman chariot and a driver and four horses (2753-1).

The specific details given for each illustration could also vary a great deal. For example, one individual was told of a French lifetime that should be illustrated not by a specific drawing but rather by a few symbols, including a cross in gold and a new moon (288-50). Conversely, another person was provided with very detailed instructions as to how she might best portray a lifetime in England:

> Above this would be depicted the humble home, only that as might be called the portion of a side wall, a little porch, with fowl—chickens, ducks and geese—all white—indicated in the yard about same. The picket fence would be shown, but not complete; not dilapidated, but as begun and not quite finished, though the posts for the runners of same would be all the way in the foreground. Not all the runners on the posts up, not all the pickets on the fence indicated. A child would be upon the step, as a girl, with a doll at the feet—but looking into the distance, where a single star would be shining–brightly. This, then, would indicate the atmosphere and a great deal of sod or green; not many trees or bushes, however.   303-31

In the description of the charts, several individuals were provided with symbols that might seem to be somewhat unusual. These include the suggestion of a brothel being included in the chart for Edgar Cayce, to depict his lifetime around Dearborn, Michigan (294-206). Another individual was told to include the drawing of three adorable fairies upon steps, depicting the qualities of love, hope, and faith (2072-7). Someone else was told to have the drawing of a hemlock leaf in her aura chart, symbolizing a family member's act of committing suicide during her Grecian incarnation (538-72). In each of the charts, symbols were apparently chosen that could best bring to the mind of the individual an awareness of the information trying to be depicted.

Although overall details of the aura chart's shape and size were generally not provided, one individual was told to create the chart as if it was a piece of parchment torn from a record (404-11). At least two others were encouraged to have their charts created to appear as an open scroll (538-72 and 993-6).

Even though the vast majority of charts contained in the Cayce files are based specifically on descriptions given in aura chart readings, it was eventually realized that it was not really necessary for an individual to have received an aura chart reading in order to have an aura chart. On at least two occasions, Esther Wynne painted aura charts for individuals based entirely upon past-life information that had been detailed in other readings (416-1 and 462-1). With this in mind, obviously individuals with a sense of one or more past lives could create a personal aura chart for themselves.

Taken together, the Cayce readings on aura charts provide a truly unique exploration of personal symbolism. Overall, an aura chart is a visual representation of a soul's lessons, attainments, failures, hardships, and developments. It can be used as a pictorial reminder of what an individual hopes to attain in the present based upon the overall soul qualities and faults that have been acquired in the past. Drawing upon the most influential lifetimes affecting the individual at the time that the chart is created, an aura chart is a material representation of a portion of the soul's Akashic Record.

Generally, a chart is read from the bottom to the top, with the most recent incarnation, as well as the ultimate spiritual ideal or highest level of attainment, situated near the top. The earliest lifetime influencing the present is most often located near the bottom of the chart. The chart is also often read from left to right, with the signs and symbols on the left representing the hopes and consciousness with which an individual came into the earth. The symbols on the right will generally correspond to the attainments, lessons, and whatever consciousness was actually cultivated during that particular period.

Just as in the case of life seals, working with an aura chart is a way of speaking to the unconscious directly. An aura chart is a material representation of the soul's individuality. The illustrations and symbols used within a chart need to create a specific awareness or correspond to a special meaning that is best known to the individual. In addition to its creative, symbolic, and philosophical appeal, an aura chart is another tool that individuals may utilize as a means of coming to know themselves.

5

Exploring the
Symbolism of Aura Charts

When Edgar Cayce gave a reading describing the creation of an aura chart, he made it clear that the symbols and pictures corresponded to experiences, lessons, talents, and shortcomings that were all part of the individual's soul history. Whether consciously or unconsciously, these symbols were to provide the individual with an awareness of information contained within the Akashic Records, or her or his soul record. Because the symbols and images corresponded to something specifically within the individual, they could facilitate self-understanding and personal development. Essentially, the chart was a pictorial representation of the soul's journey through its most significant lifetimes and the corresponding experiences and development of consciousness that could be attributed to each incarnation:

> As we have given, an aura chart is the attempt to inter-

> pret the material experiences of individuals in their jour-
> neys through the earth; indicating, pictorially, as to that
> place in the earth of the individual activity, and—upon
> either the right or the left—the sources from which the
> entity came into activity in the earthly or material con-
> sciousness. About same is symbolized, in the signs of the
> zodiac, as to that portion of body which was stressed
> through that particular period of activity.   5746-1

Because every soul has experienced a personal journey through history that is entirely unique, each individual will have different feelings and personal responses to various cultures, countries, historical epochs, and life experiences. The symbols and pictures that are part of an aura chart have a specific meaning for the individual to whom the chart belongs that does not necessarily correspond to what other individuals may think of the very same symbols. For that reason, a contemporary aura chart created by an individual would be made up of symbols and illustrations most meaningful to that individual.

In the same manner that Cayce gave life readings, dealing with the topic of reincarnation, the aura chart readings were given to individuals to help them understand soul strengths and weaknesses, as well as their own potentials and challenges. Even though the charts often provided information regarding how a soul had both "gained" and "lost" in terms of soul development, the readings stated that faults should be minimized and strengths magnified as a means of becoming the most helpful influence in the life of the individual. The charts provided by the Cayce readings also described the ultimate attainment that could be reached by the individual as well as how that individual might best realize his or her relationship to the Whole.

As a means of familiarizing individuals with the appearance of a variety of aura charts and their corresponding interpretation, a number of charts from the Cayce files have been included. Each of the following aura charts provides some background information on the person to whom the chart belongs, as well as an interpretation of what some of the symbols and images might have meant to that individual.

Aura Chart for Mrs. [2390]
Image 13: Painted by Esther Wynne

BACKGROUND: Mrs. [2390] was a housewife who also worked as a bookkeeper and auditor. She and her husband were both interested in the work of Edgar Cayce. Over a period of three years, Mrs. [2390] had nine readings, including several life readings; a reading on business advice; readings for health problems, including anemia and a pelvic problem; and an aura chart reading. She had a son in 1946 at the age of thirty-six.

According to the readings, the lifetimes that were affecting her most in the present included incarnations in Atlantis, ancient Egypt, Persia, Palestine, eighteenth-century America and England, and nineteenth-century America.

GENERAL INTERPRETATION OF MRS. [2390]'S AURA CHART: THE CREATION/ATLANTIS ILLUSTRATION:

According to the Cayce readings, during an incarnation in Atlantis, Mrs. [2390] was a priestess in Atlantis who learned to be of great service to others. In fact, her selfless devotion to every class of society became so well known that she was elevated almost to the point of being worshiped by some of the people.

The central picture at the bottom depicts a lotus flower blooming atop a mucky pool of water, suggesting the birth of an individual soul from out of the substance of a primordial universe. In order to further illustrate this being the time of Creation, Cayce suggested that two faces should be drawn coming out of the flower, as well as a complete figure becoming an individual soul. The inverted pyramid over the figure's head symbolizes the act of spirit entering matter. Upon the left of the central illustration was to be drawn a cross and upon the right an anchor—representative of spirituality or being anchored in the ultimate ideal.

On the lower left is drawn a symbol that is supposed to be the geographic outline of Atlantis. On the lower right is drawn the astrological symbol for the earth. This suggests coming in to Atlantis and leaving that incarnation having acquired traits associated with materiality. However, the presence of the anchor and the cross suggests that Mrs. [2390] retained her connection to the divine at this point in her soul's journey.

THE ANCIENT EGYPTIAN ILLUSTRATION:

During a lifetime in ancient Egypt, Mrs. [2390] had once again assumed the role of priestess. For a time she assisted the high priest Ra Ta in healing, guiding, and training individuals in two of the predominant temples of the time: the Temple of Sacrifice, associated with physical purification and healing, and the Temple Beautiful, associated with mental-spiritual training and transformation. During this incarnation, Mrs. [2390] apparently made great strides in her own spiritual development. The readings suggest, however, that there also came a time during this period when she abandoned her devotion to serving others.

The central illustration corresponding to this lifetime depicts a woman seated upon the ground with an elderly man resting his head in her lap. The readings indicate that the elderly man (the high priest) is speaking to the woman and foretelling events that will transpire in the earth. In the background can be seen a crescent moon on the horizon, symbolizing the passage of time and the influence of feminine energies. Twelve stars and a cross fill the sky, suggesting that one of the things that the priest is foretelling is the time of Jesus and the Apostles.

To the left of the figures is a picture of the Sphinx, representing the ancient mysteries of Egypt. On the right, illustrations depicting the Temple of Sacrifice and the Temple Beautiful exist side-by-side. To complete the Egyptian picture, Cayce suggested including a picture of a camel, which would provide a counterbalance to the illustration of the Sphinx.

The planetary and astrological symbols located just below the Egyptian illustration on either side correspond to the abilities and the consciousness associated with the soul. The readings advised placing the symbol for Mercury (in blue and gold) on the left, surrounded by four symbols of Cancer. This might suggest that the soul came into the earth with great wisdom and mental abilities (Mercury), as well as enormous sensitivity and emotional feelings (Cancer).

On the right-hand side, corresponding to the consciousness attained and what was actually learned during that incarnation, the readings suggested the symbol for Venus[3] surrounded by Leo. This could indicate that the soul further developed an appreciation for love and beauty (Venus), while maintaining a consciousness of openness and broadmindedness toward others (Leo).

THE PERSIAN ILLUSTRATION:

Continuing in her personal soul development, during a lifetime in Persia, [2390] had apparently been an influence for much good. During a period of invasion by the Greeks, she held fast to her commitment to healing and to spiritual principles and tenets that had become a part of her life. Of wise council, she provided much assistance to all that listened to her. She even helped many of the invaders change their allegiance. Cayce suggested that she had been one of those who had truly "aided in turning the tide," so that the Persian city prevailed and the invasion came to naught.

The central picture is an illustration of a woman looking after the needs of others that are ill. Cayce described these individuals as one being bound at the lower limbs, another having an injury to the head, and a third being handed something to drink. It was suggested that the woman be clothed in white, indicating her angelic ministry to others. On each side of this illustration, Cayce suggested positioning a small circle. The circle on the left contains the letters "EL," undoubtedly corresponding to the divine, and the circle on the right contains the letters "DI" in gold. (Cayce did not explain what DI represented, either symbolically or to Mrs. [2390] personally.)

The planetary symbol on the left is Jupiter and it is surrounded by the sign of Aries. Jupiter can correspond to possessing broadness of vision and Aries might suggest that [2390] entered that experience with a capacity for leading others. Saturn is on the right and Pisces surrounds it. This could suggest that the soul achieved personal self-

---

[3]On occasion Esther Wynne erroneously painted an incorrect astrological symbol when something else had been suggested by the readings. For example, she often mistakenly painted the symbol for Taurus whenever Venus had been suggested.

discipline during that period (Saturn), while maintaining humility and a devotion to spiritual truths (Pisces).

THE PALESTINIAN ILLUSTRATION:

The readings told [2390] that she had experienced a lifetime in the Promised Land during the period of the early Church. Reportedly, she had been the sister of one of the early bishops, Lucius, who was head of the church at Laodicea. At the time she had apparently disputed with Paul because—contrary to the apostle's belief—she maintained that it was possible to be practical in things of a worldly nature while still being committed to spiritual truths. Her reading stated that at the time she had also witnessed the speaking of tongues during Pentecost, in which each listener heard the apostles in their own language (Acts 2). Because of that experience, all kinds of spiritual and psychic phenomenon were of interest to her in the present.

The illustration suggested for this period in her soul's journey was to be a duplication of Leonardo da Vinci's "Last Supper," when the apostles were gathered together with Jesus in the upper room. In addition to what da Vinci had painted, the picture was to include a heart above the head of Jesus. This picture corresponds to the central influences that these individuals had over the life of [2390] during that period.

On the left is painted three figures in a small boat upon a turbulent sea. This probably indicates some of the challenges that faced [2390] as a member of a small sect, setting sail on a new spiritual journey. On the right is a speaker in a small church, with individuals from the congregation all listening to what is being said. This would correspond to the way in which the early Church spread its tenets by speaking to individuals and small groups.

The planetary symbol of Neptune is on the left, surrounded by Libra. Neptune could indicate that she entered the earth possessing traits associated with mysticism and spiritual insight. Libra might correspond to idealism and balance. On the right is Mars, surrounded by Sagittarius. In part, this suggests that she was prone to action and may have possessed the ability to defend others (Mars). Sagittarius can be associated with a consciousness of optimism.

THE EIGHTEENTH-CENTURY AMERICA AND ENGLAND ILLUSTRATION:

The readings make it clear that the lifetime in which Mrs. [2390] had exhibited the greatest amount of selfishness had occurred in the eighteenth century, when she had been Marge Oglethorpe. A relative (daughter?/niece?) of James Oglethorpe (1696-1785), who had been a member of the British Parliament and the first governor of Georgia, Mrs. [2390] was told that during this lifetime she thought herself to be "just a little bit better than anybody else." (2390-9) Cayce said that at the time she "looked down on everyone except on Marge." In addition, she was also involved in numerous questionable escapades with members of the opposite sex. Eventually, however, after the family had returned to England, the readings suggest that she experienced numerous personal trials, causing her to turn to religion and transforming many of the negative characteristics within herself.

The illustration associated with this lifetime was to depict a "misty figure" walking through a peach orchard in bloom, perhaps indicating the act of spending much time alone in thought. In an oval on the left, a horse drawn carriage shows an individual with a parasol who Cayce said needed to appear lax and self-indulgent. Both the central illustration and the picture on the left seem to indicate someone who thinks only of self.

The picture in the oval on the right depicts an individual kneeling before a church altar, staring upward toward a crucifix. This image symbolizes Mrs. [2390]'s involvement in religion that occurred at the time as a means of dealing with her personal trials.

Cayce suggested that the planetary symbol on the left was to be the earth, suggesting her material concerns. The earth is surrounded by the sign for Sagittarius which, in addition to optimism, can indicate personal restlessness and being prone to extremes. The readings advised the placement of the moon on the right with "a face in same" and to have this surrounded by the symbol of Libra. The moon can symbolize getting in touch with feminine energies and Libra was suggested for its representation of balance.

THE NINETEENTH-CENTURY AMERICA ILLUSTRATION:

According to the readings, part of Mrs. [2390]'s attraction to the Cayce work was due to a very short lifetime she had experienced just prior to the present. Cayce stated that she had been his older sister, Leila Cayce, who had died on August 24, 1876, at the age of two-and-a-half-years-old—seven months before Cayce's own birth. Interestingly enough, Mrs. [2390] had been born exactly thirty-four years to the day of Leila's death: August 24, 1910! In spite of the shortness of her life, the readings suggest that the death of this child had caused the Cayce family to deepen their faith in God as a means of dealing with the experience.

The central picture depicts an old two-story, southern-style home with columns. The readings suggested putting an individual on the porch staring toward the west and seeing a vision of Egypt, suggesting the continuation of the Egyptian influence that had been prominent in Cayce's own past life as well as those who were intimately involved in his work. On the near left is the letter "G," undoubtedly referring to God, placed within a triangle, which is suggestive of Egypt as well as transformation. On the near right, a crucifix was to be placed within a circle, representing the influence of the Christ as well as spirituality in general.

In regards to planetary symbols, the symbols on the far left and far right were to be the same: the symbol of Mercury surrounded by the sign of Pisces. Mercury is often associated with the mental influence, personal seeking, and even meditation. Pisces can correspond to humility and a commitment to spiritual truths.

POSSIBLE ATTAINMENTS ILLUSTRATION:

The final symbols suggested for Mrs. [2390]'s aura chart included a cross with a cornucopia on either side. In each of the cornucopias was to be drawn seven vials, corresponding to the fruits of the spirit. The image suggests personal attainments and mastery that can be a part of her soul experience as she relies upon the promises of the Christ. Above this image is the all-seeing eye, which can correspond to singleness of vision, the ideal, and the presence of the divine.

Aura Chart for Mr. [533]
Image 14: Painted by Esther Wynne

BACKGROUND: While in his early twenties, Mr. [533] complained of severe abdominal problems. In order to treat the condition, doctors mistakenly removed his appendix when the condition was actually due to an intestinal obstruction. As a result he continued to deteriorate until his mother brought him to Edgar Cayce in 1934. Over a period of eight years, he would have twenty readings. Nineteen of his readings were health related due to his problems with colitis, gastritis, and inflammation of the intestines. He would eventually be cured of the condition. Mr. [533] also had one aura chart reading.

In time, he would become an auto salesman, marry, and have a son. Because of the effectiveness of the readings, he became a financial supporter of Cayce's work. Both his wife and son received readings, as well. According to the readings, the lifetimes that were affecting him most in the present included incarnations in ancient Egypt, Persia, Rome, and Colonial America.

GENERAL INTERPRETATION OF MR. [533]'S AURA CHART: THE EGYPTIAN ILLUSTRATION:

Although Mr. [533] did not have a personal life reading of his own, it is possible to surmise some of his past-life experiences from his aura chart reading as well as from the life readings for his wife and son. In Egypt he may have been most involved in writing, vocational guidance for others, and transportation.

The aura chart reading for [533] suggests starting with a wheel in the center at the bottom of the chart. The wheel was described as being simplistic in design, consisting of only a rim and four spokes that might bring to mind his interest during that period in various modes of transportation. The plant to the left of the wheel is a papyrus branch, corresponding to the type of paper used for writing at the time. The tree to the right is an apple tree, which Cayce said would symbolize the helpfulness of his vocational activities during that period.

The planetary symbol on the left is Venus, surrounded by Aries.

This might suggest his appreciation for beauty and his being adept at making friends (Venus)–useful skills in providing others with guidance and direction (Aries). Upon the right is the symbol for Jupiter, surrounded by Sagittarius. Cayce said that this combination specifically indicated, "the mental building up of the universal consciousness as indicated in Jupiter, but with a purposefulness of a self-interest in the activity." (533-20)

THE PERSIAN ILLUSTRATION:

The next most influential incarnation in Mr. [533]'s soul development occurred in ancient Persia, when [533] was a merchant traveler. At the time he was apparently headstrong and prone to extremes in terms of his moods for he possessed the tendency to be either very somber and depressed or very enthusiastic and cheerful.

The illustration shows the leader of a caravan with two camels in the foreground and nine following close behind. Each of the camels is laden with merchant wares, traveling toward a commercial center at the time that Cayce called the "city in the hills and the plains." The city can be seen off in the distance on the left side of the picture.

The planetary symbol on the left is Uranus, which the readings indicated would symbolize the extremes that [533] possessed as a soul. It is surrounded by the sign of Leo, corresponding to the strength, virility, and "headstrongness" that were all a part of the individual's consciousness. The attainments for that incarnation were indicated as being best symbolized by Venus (an appreciation for love and beauty) surrounded by Libra (balance).

THE ROMAN ILLUSTRATION:

The Roman experience was one in which [533] was a slave for a time, forced to fight with beasts in the arena for the amusement of the Roman people. At one point he became critically injured and was apparently healed by a member of the small Christian sect. The healing provided him with a new perspective on life and he became a convert to the new religion.

The picture depicts a Roman guard leading three slaves in chains. Cayce suggested that in spite of their imprisonment the slaves were to appear proud "even of their bonds." To the left of the Roman guard is two golden stars (symbolizing ideals, influences, or attainments) and above the stars is an olive branch, representing peace and the Christ influence. On the right are two blue stars with the cup of the Eucharist above, perhaps symbolizing the influence of the early Church and the Christ.

On the lower left is the planetary symbol for Venus (love and beauty) surrounded by the sign of Pisces (commitment to spiritual truths). The planetary symbol on the lower right is Mercury (mental influences and personal seeking) surrounded by Aries, which could indicate that he became a leadership influence in converting others to the spiritual truths he had discovered.

THE COLONIAL AMERICA ILLUSTRATION:

The readings suggest that throughout the period just before and during the American Revolution, Mr. [533] was a blacksmith in one of the colonies.

The illustration shows a blacksmith with his hammer and anvil standing near an open furnace, working on a wheel. The readings suggested putting a very rugged cross to the left of the blacksmith, perhaps symbolizing the religious influence of the day. On the right was to be placed a rooster, which may have a variety of possible meanings. The rooster can symbolize male arrogance, the denial of the Christ, or it might simply suggest the end of a period.

Once again the Mercurian influence appears as the planetary symbol on the lower left, suggesting strong mental abilities. It is surrounded by Sagittarius, which can correspond to adaptability, optimism, or being prone to self-interests. On the lower right is the symbol for Mars, which might correspond to a pioneering spirit, as well as to what Cayce indicated as a "temper" during this period. It is surrounded by the sign of Scorpio (persistence and determination, as well as a sense of purposefulness).

POSSIBLE ATTAINMENTS ILLUSTRATION:

The uppermost symbols suggested for Mr. [533]'s aura chart included a cornucopia in the center with a cross on either side. Coming out of the cornucopia was to be painted seven stones, including an agate, a diamond, a ruby, a pearl, and an amethyst, which the readings indicated would symbolize the virtues of "meekness, temperance, love, faith, hope, patience, etc." Finally, on either side was to be placed a cross, which was described as follows: "Both of these would be in gold and white, one upon the left and one upon the right. This indicates the attainment in plenty through patience, love, hope, faith, as in the Cross crowning thy efforts, and in keeping the faith. This we find the aura chart of the entity, [533]."

Aura Chart for Gertrude Cayce
Image 15: Painted by Esther Wynne

BACKGROUND: Gertrude Cayce was Edgar Cayce's wife and the most frequent conductor of the readings. A housewife and mother with two sons, she was known for her stability and her love of home and family. Throughout her marriage to Edgar Cayce, she would have a total of seventy-two readings on every imaginable topic: health, past lives, mental-spiritual advice, dreams, business advice, and personal guidance. Her final reading was an aura chart reading given in 1942.

At the time of her aura chart reading, her most influential incarnations are depicted by two illustrations symbolizing Egypt, an image associated with Persia, and several symbols indicating a Grecian incarnation.

GENERAL INTERPRETATION OF GERTRUDE CAYCE'S AURA CHART: THE EGYPTIAN ILLUSTRATIONS:

As is evidenced by Mrs. Cayce's aura chart, her Egyptian incarnation played a major role in her soul development. The readings suggest that she was a favorite dancer of the pharaoh and eventually fell in love with the high priest, Ra Ta. The alliance between the two eventually resulted in the banishment of both. At the time, she apparently possessed a tremendous intellect, and after the period of banishment was over and she and the high priest returned to Egypt, she became revered by the people for her wisdom and her depth of spiritual awareness. It seems apparent that the two Egyptian illustrations correspond to the two unique periods Gertrude Cayce had in Egypt during that lifetime—the first as a temple dancer prior to the banishment and the second as the companion of Ra Ta and a teacher in her own right after the banishment had come to an end.

The readings advised creating the aura chart to appear as an opening scroll, perhaps suggesting that only a portion of the Akashic Record for this soul had been portrayed. The bottommost picture is described as the outline of a pyramid off in the distance with birds flying about the structure. In addition to the Egyptian lifetime overall, the pyramid is associated with spiritual knowledge and transformation, and birds can represent higher truths as well as thoughts and ideas. The illustration also includes a palm tree and a well in the left foreground, which might correspond to this soul's humble beginnings early on, and the tip of the rising sun in the background on the right, which could represent the dawn of a new experience.

The readings advised Gertrude that her soul possessed a tremendous capacity for knowledge and mental understanding, which is obviously portrayed by the symbol of Mercury on the left. It is surrounded by the sign of Aquarius, probably associated with the consciousness of humanitarianism, for which she would eventually become known in that incarnation. A five-pointed star on top, which the readings associate with humanity, and an eight-pointed star at the bottom, which can correspond to attainment, also border these symbols.

The planetary symbol on the right is Jupiter (broadness of vision) and the sign of Libra (balance) surrounds it. The readings suggest that taken together these symbols portray that the soul attained balance and liberation. Once again these images are bordered by an eight-pointed star on the bottom and a five-pointed star at the top.

The second Egyptian illustration contains an image of the goddess Isis, holding the child Horus. Cayce stated that this image was to represent the soul's interest and developments in terms of motherhood and children and the activities related to both. On the left side of Isis is a large sheaf of wheat, which the readings stated would indicate abundance. Undoubtedly pertaining to physical, mental, and spiritual abundance because of the soul's position and attainments at this time. The readings also advised placing a red sickle next to the wheat as a symbol of wrath. Apparently, the soul had become angry because her banishment had not only exiled her from Egypt for a time but also because one of her children had died because of the banishment.

To the right of Isis is the entrance to a home, associated with this soul's emphasis on family life. In front of the home is the Egyptian flax plant, which the readings described as indicating strength. Finally, three sets of five-pointed stars were to be placed on either side of Isis. The three stars were to be aligned in the shape of a pyramid, indicating Egypt as well as the balance of body-mind-spirit. The stars were said to also represent the soul's strengths and purposefulness throughout that experience.

THE PERSIAN ILLUSTRATION:

According to the Cayce readings during a period in ancient Persia, Gertrude Cayce was abandoned as a child and became the adopted daughter of Uhjltd (Edgar Cayce), a prominent healer and desert leader. As she grew to adulthood in this "city in the hills and plains," she would become a teacher and leader of young people, providing them with a new understanding of the divine that was being promulgated at the time. The readings suggest that one of the things she learned in this incarnation was patience and persistence.

The illustration for this period depicts two columns with a doorway opening up to a beautiful desert vista and the rising sun just beyond. This image plus the letters "EL," which were to be painted over the doorway, can all represent a new understanding of God and the overreaching divine influence in the affairs of humankind.

Upon the left is the planetary symbol for Uranus, which can indicate the soul's independence and strength during this period. The attainment portrayed by the planetary symbol on the right is Saturn, associated with patience and personal self-discipline.

THE GRECIAN ILLUSTRATION:

The readings suggest that Gertrude's greatest drive for knowledge and understanding in the present came as a result of her having been one of the daughters of Socrates. The lifetime, however, had been one of great hardship due to the bickering of her parents and her father's inability to support a family, preferring instead to act as a philosopher to young students. In addition to her material lack, she also experienced persecution after her father's sentence of suicide was carried out (due to the state finding him a dangerous influence on the youth). The readings suggested somberly that because of her challenging experiences her soul had failed to fully utilize all the knowledge she had acquired in that experience.

Three images were suggested to represent the soul's experiences during that lifetime: a goblet in the center, a hemlock leaf on the left, and a scroll ("with fine lines of gold") on the right (538-72). Obviously the hemlock leaf represents the poisoning of her father. The scroll is associated with the knowledge and understanding that were available to her during that period. The cup can indicate several things, including the literal cup that Socrates drank from to kill himself or metaphorically it might represent her own potential mission and life's path at the time.

The planetary symbol on the left was to be Mercury (mental abilities), surrounded by the sign of Sagittarius, which in this case might indicate the soul's being prone to self-interests. On the right is Venus (love and beauty) and it is surrounded by Pisces (spiritual truths).

POSSIBLE ATTAINMENTS ILLUSTRATION:

The final symbols suggested for Gertrude Cayce's aura chart included a crown (attainment of spiritual truths) adorned with seven stars (the fruits of the spirit, spiritual perfection, and the seven centers). Below the crown was to be the face of the Christ Child, corresponding to the birth of the Christ Consciousness. Atop the crown was to be a torch of fire, suggestive of knowledge and lighting the way for others. On either side of the crown are seven lighted candles, corresponding to the enlightenment of the seven spiritual centers. On either side above the candles was to be placed a crucifix, which the readings stated in this arrangement would indicate an attempt to measure up to the light of the cross (selfless spirituality).

Aura Chart for Mr. [462]
Image 16: Painted by Esther Wynne

BACKGROUND: Mr. [462] was a forty-five-year-old sea captain when he had a life reading in 1929. Over the next fourteen years he would have a total of eighteen readings dealing with subjects related to health, business advice, and vocational guidance in addition to his life reading. He and his wife were also involved in the Study Group work that explored spiritual growth and development and resulted in the publication of *A Search for God*. Although he never had an aura chart reading from Edgar Cayce, his wife had one, and he eventually requested that Esther Wynne paint him a chart based on his own life reading.

According to his life reading, the most notable incarnations having an influence upon Mr. [462] at the time of the reading included an ancient Native American incarnation, a lifetime in Egypt, an incarnation upon the Greek isle of Crete, and a lifetime in Norway.

GENERAL INTERPRETATION OF MR. [462]'S AURA CHART: THE ANCIENT NATIVE AMERICA ILLUSTRATION:

According to the Cayce readings, Mr. [462] was a Native American who lived in the mountainous regions of the western portion of what is now the United States. At the time, his bravery and power led him to become a ruler over five tribes. Unfortunately, his elevation to leadership caused him to become tyrannical in nature, and he eventually lost spiritually as a result. Because of this incarnation, in the present he possessed a love of history and an attraction to this same geographical portion of the United States.

The illustration depicts a Native American ruler speaking with representatives of the five tribes for which he is responsible. On the left is the earth, which can correspond to the material world. It also portrays the North American continent, which is the location of this particular incarnation.

On the right is the planetary symbol of Mars, which can be associated with a pioneering spirit and being prone to action and power. It is surrounded by the symbol of Leo, perhaps indicating his own tendencies at the time toward being willful and headstrong.

THE EGYPTIAN ILLUSTRATION:

During a period in ancient Egypt, Mr. [462] was a native Egyptian who was among the people subdued by a conquering nation. Although appearing to go along with the conquering peoples, the readings suggest that [462] maintained his spirit of rebellion and waited for the right opportunity to fight against his oppressors. Apparently, his rebellion was based on ego because the Egyptian country had actually prospered under the change. For that reason, for a time he digressed spiritually. However, he eventually changed his allegiance in support of the new rulers and became a leader in his own right and a champion of the spiritual principles being promulgated throughout the country. Mr. [462]'s interest in things of a spiritual nature was traced to this period in his soul's history.

The picture shows two figures, presumably an Egyptian high priest in the center and the native Egyptian on the right. Off to the left is the Great Pyramid and the Sphinx can be seen in the background. Overhead is a five-pointed star, which indicates his own attainment after his personal transformation. On the right is the moon, corresponding to the passage of time and his own growth in terms of the unconscious. The surrounding stars can indicate attainments as well as the fact that he became a guiding light and source of direction in his position of leadership.

THE GRECIAN ILLUSTRATION:

During a lifetime corresponding to a period of the Greek Empire, Mr. [462] was a citizen of the isle of Crete and apparently in a position of authority. When it became clear that Greeks from the mainland wished to overrun the island, Mr. [462] was one of those who defended the native people. His success eventually resulted in his being elevated to a position of greater authority—a position he would misuse through the selfish aggrandizement of power. Eventually, he was both banished and imprisoned. The readings stated that from this period [462] had gained a dislike of prison walls for they often led to the "belittling of the inner man." (462-1)

The central picture shows a ruler being surrounded by wealth, food, and drink—suggesting that this position of power eventually turned to the satisfying of his own needs. On the left is an outline of the island of Crete. On the right is the picture of an old man with a cane being held in his jail cell, corresponding to the period in this incarnation when Mr. [462] fell from his position of leadership and became imprisoned.

The planetary symbol and astrological sign on the far right is once again a picture of Mars, only this time it is surrounded by the sign of Capricorn. The readings suggest that in this incarnation Mr. [462] gained in his understanding of power, corresponding to Mars. Unfortunately, however, the latter portion of his life was filled only with discontent, which can be indicated by the sign of Capricorn.

THE NORWEGIAN ILLUSTRATION:

Mr. [462]'s talent as a sea captain could be traced to a lifetime in Norway. There he had been among those who had journeyed toward "western shores," eventually coming to England. During that period he acquired both daring and fearlessness that he retained in the present. He also made great spiritual progress during that incarnation and gained in soul development because of his ability to become committed to a higher ideal, helping himself and providing a living example to others in the process.

The central picture depicts a Norwegian sailing vessel journeying toward the west. On the right is the symbol for Mercury, surrounded by the sign of Libra. Mercury can correspond to personal seeking, for it is often associated with mental influences, the mind, and wisdom. In addition to balance, in this instance Libra might also represent his growth in idealism and diplomacy. On the left is Venus (appreciation for love and beauty) and it is surrounded by Sagittarius (lover or exploring and freedom).

POSSIBLE ATTAINMENTS ILLUSTRATION:

The final symbols that Esther Wynne painted in Mr. [462]'s aura chart include an eight-pointed star, symbolizing attainment, and a cross on the left and the right, which generally corresponds to the ultimate guiding influence or ideal. The Bible in the center is open to the passage "Lo, I am with you" (Matthew 28:20), as a reminder of the ever-present presence of the divine. Finally, a six-pointed star is located at the top of the chart, associated with spiritual community (e.g., the Star of David) as well as divine love.

6

Creating Your Own
Aura Chart

Since an aura chart is a visual depiction of a soul's history and its experiences, lessons, achievements, and shortcomings through time, one of the requirements for creating your own aura chart is to gain an awareness of possible past lives. For some individuals, an awareness of the past has already occurred through psychic readings, dreams, personal intuition, an attraction to certain periods in history, personal regressions, and so forth. For others, even if the knowledge of personal past lives is not yet known, a few simple exercises can bring a rudimentary knowledge of the past to conscious awareness.

The purpose of an aura chart is to help facilitate self-awareness. The Cayce readings also advised individuals that ultimately a chart should magnify an individual's strengths and minimize her or his weaknesses. Although it might be helpful, in reality artistic talent is not required to create your own aura chart. In addition to sketching or painting, an individual might simply decide to utilize pictures, images, and symbols clipped from magazines. Remember, an aura chart is a method of self-discovery that utilizes symbolism. It will not necessarily be seen by anyone else. In discussing the purpose, creation, and appearance of a chart, Cayce told one person:

> In analyzing such a drawing from such charts, much as to the beauty of same–as we have indicated–depends upon the artist.
>
> That there is the attempt to minimize the faults and magnify the virtues should be the policy, the experience not only of the artist but from those influences that would indicate to an entity symbols or figures as might give the concept of the entity's experiences through varied sojourns in the earth...
>
> Hence (for the entity's interpretation of same), let that as becomes a visualization of same ever be towards the more helpful, the more hopeful or the spiritual interpretation of the characters and symbols as may be here indicated.   2378-2

In creating an aura chart, individuals will be attempting to get in touch with the soul's memory. The process of pulling the chart together is simply the act of bringing that memory to conscious awareness. The Edgar Cayce readings suggest that aura charts are ultimately a symbolic representation of a person's individuality. These charts can be helpful in gaining an overall awareness of an individual's soul experiences, ideals, and level of consciousness through various activities as well as one's overall relationship to others. Oftentimes, they also depict the ultimate ideal or personal attainment that can be achieved by the individual as he or she focuses on the importance of soul development.

Cayce suggested that as an individual takes the time to reflect upon a personal chart, the pictures and symbols could bring to mind the awareness of strengths and weaknesses as well as one's ultimate direction. The level of complexity used in aura charts is really up to the individual and his or her understanding of symbolism. For example, although the readings often provided detailed descriptions and even utilized the symbols of the planets to correspond to the attainment of specific lessons and the signs of the zodiac to indicate the corresponding level of consciousness development, the use of specific types of symbols is entirely up to the individual. What is important is to utilize those symbols that will best portray whatever information is trying to be brought to mind. For that reason, the charts for some individuals could be filled with complex symbols and images that cannot be understood by anyone else. Others, however, might simply decide to use photocopied pictures from magazines and history books that appear relatively easy to decipher.

Once an aura chart has been created, an individual might reflect upon that chart regularly as a reminder of his or her purposes, strengths, weaknesses, and direction. It can be a tool for personal understanding and guidance. When an individual reflects upon the chart, it can become an inspirational means of evaluating how well the individual is doing in overcoming past faults and utilizing inner strengths as well as being a reminder of the soul's ultimate desire.

The following information may be helpful in calling to mind past lives and personal strengths and weaknesses that you possess in the present—information that can be useful in creating an aura chart. To begin, you might wish to pull together the "Materials needed to create your aura chart." Afterwards, you may wish to review the following lists: "Things that can be helpful to remember in creating your aura chart" and "Possible methods of obtaining symbols and past-life information for aura charts." There is also an aura chart relaxation reverie, "A Journey into Your Imagination," that may be useful in gathering past-life information and symbols for the creation of your personal aura chart.

Materials needed to create your aura chart:
- White cardboard or rectangular heavy-weight white paper that is perhaps 81/2 inches wide by 14 inches long
- A vertical rectangular or the shape of a scroll drawn on the cardboard
- Colored pencils, crayons, paints, or watercolors (or a variety of

magazines that you can use to cut out appropriate pictures and then glue them onto your aura chart)

Things that can be helpful to remember in creating your aura chart:
(In other words, what kinds of pictures, symbols, colors, images, or even words could be helpful in calling some of these things to mind?)
- Things that remind you of historical epochs or cultures you are attracted to
- Things that remind you of historical epochs or cultures that you do not like
- Things that remind you of your positive thoughts and opinions of others
- Things that remind you of your negative thoughts and opinions of others
- Things that you would like to develop within yourself
- Things that you would like to change within yourself
- Things that you are good at
- Things that you enjoy doing
- Things that are challenging
- Things you need to work on
- Things that are a part of your purpose
- Things that will make your life more balanced

Possible methods of obtaining symbols and past-life information for aura charts:
- Using guided imagery (see "Aura Chart Relaxation and Reverie")
- Obtaining a psychic reading or a hypnotic regression
- Recalling historical periods, cultures, geographic areas, art and architecture, ethnic foods, and clothing that you have strong opinions about (positive as well as negative)
- Recalling what subjects were easy for you in school
- Recalling personal experiences with déjà vu
- Trying meditation and relaxation
- Calling to mind reoccurring dream images and symbols
- Listening to inspirational music
- Thinking of your own aspirations, hopes, and ideals
- Working with inspirational writing

- Working with movement or dance
- Calling to mind your talents and abilities
- Thinking of your favorite colors
- Recalling places or images that remind you of special memories from your life
- Working with your own intuition
- Considering what reoccurring patterns and experiences may have tried to teach you in your present life
- Listing symbols that remind you of your favorite activities
- Reading from scriptures or uplifting verse
- Contemplating whether your body's markings—moles, birthmarks, etc.—can tell you anything about yourself
- Taking time for introspection and self-analysis (e.g., considering such things as what you need to develop in yourself, what you need to change, etc.)
- Considering what other people have described as your personal strengths and weaknesses
- Reflecting upon your memories as a child, especially in terms of what you wanted to be when you grew older
- Reflecting upon your childhood fears, interests, hobbies, and worries
- Remembering any designs/shapes that you seem drawn to
- Considering whether you habitually make any persistent doodles
- Pondering the astrological (and/or numerological) influences that are most influential in your life
- Contemplating your life's purpose or mission in life

A JOURNEY INTO YOUR IMAGINATION: AURA CHART RELAXATION AND REVERIE

Note: A reverie is best done with another person (reading the reverie like a script), or with oneself first narrating the reverie on a tape and then playing it back in order to experience the exercise. Reveries are generally narrated at about one-third the normal rate of speech.

NARRATION:

Aura Chart Reverie:

Get comfortable in your chair (or lie down) and close your eyes. Take a deep breath and tell yourself to relax. Take another deep breath—breathing in relaxation and calm and slowly breathing out any tension or stress. If there is some part of your body that needs to relax, tense up the muscles in that area and hold it, hold it, and then relax. Take another deep breath and relax. [Pause.]

As you become more comfortable and relaxed, focus your attention on your breathing. Let your awareness begin to notice how the air feels cool as you inhale and how it feels warm as you breathe out. Continue to breathe and relax. Breathe in this cool sense of relaxation all through your body. Remain comfortable and very much at peace. Listen to the sound of my voice and relax. Simply breathe in relaxation. [Pause.]

Imagine that your breath is a beautiful white light, constantly filling your body and bringing you into a deeper sense of peace. Let the light of relaxation move through your feet . . . Let it move through your legs and hips . . . Let it flow through your chest, back and arms . . . Let it relax your shoulders, your neck, your head, and your forehead . . . Finally, let it spread through your entire body, leaving you totally at peace and very much relaxed. [Pause.]

This will be an experience where you will remain in control. You are going to let your mind wander back in time, to a safe place, before the present. As an objective observer, you are going to have the opportunity to witness experiences and activities from your soul's past. You won't need to make any special effort, just relax and let your imagination flow. Totally relaxed and totally detached, you will be able to observe some of your most meaningful experiences from long ago. You will see them clearly in your imagination with a feeling of total safety and security. Relax into your imagination and let yourself feel relaxed and totally at peace . . . [Pause.]

I am going to count from one to seven, and with each number I want you to visualize yourself descending one step at a time into a place of safety where you will be able to encounter memories as an objective observer . . . One—take the first step, feeling completely relaxed . . .

Two, three, four—you remain very much in control and aware of the activities of your mind . . . Five and six—take the final and seventh step into the resources of your personal memory . . . You are now in a state of relaxation, very much at peace and aware of the sound of my voice . . . Now, imagine yourself as a soul, having the opportunity to witness the record of your personal journey.

Take a deep breath and feel comfortable. In your imagination, I want you to see one of the earliest soul's memories that you have. This is an important memory where you can see yourself sitting beside a body of water, a lake, a pond, any body of water with a sparkling smooth surface. Just relax and become an observer of this scene.

Slowly, ever so slowly, the surroundings of this place come into focus . . . you can see the scenery around you. With greater and greater clarity, you can see the surroundings, the sky, the ground, and the body of water . . . all as it appeared in this long ago past . . . [Pause.]

Now, in your imagination, I want you to gaze into the water and see what you look like? How does your face appear? Are you a male or a female? Are you young or are you old? Can you tell what you're wearing? What does it feel like to be who you are . . . here in this long ago past? Make a mental note of who you are . . . and what you seem to be doing . . . [Pause.]

Look around at the scenery . . . what does it look like? Do you see grass . . . or soil . . . or trees . . . or mountains . . . or desert sand? Can you feel the warmth of the sun upon your face or are there clouds and wind? Can you feel the mood of this place? Make a mental note of what you see and feel. Do you see other buildings or structures? Are there animals or people around you? If you have difficulty seeing, simply try to hear or feel this place. Let the memories come forward and make a mental note of what you see, hear, or feel . . . [Pause.]

Next in your imagination, I want you to see if you can recall what your purpose was in that incarnation? In other words, what did you come into the earth to accomplish? [Pause.] What talents or abilities did you bring to that lifetime? [Pause.] Was anything left undone? [Pause.] If you can, imagine what other people might have said during that period about your greatest strengths and your greatest weaknesses? [Pause.] Are there any symbols or pictures that can remind you of this experience in your soul's journey? [Pause.] Are there any symbols that can remind you of the strengths you came in with or the weaknesses you hoped to overcome? [Pause.] Is there a symbol or a sign that can represent what you learned during that lifetime or the consciousness you actually attained? [Pause.] What about this incarnation is most important to you in the present day? [Pause.]

Next, in your imagination, I want you to visualize an enormous movie screen standing before your eyes. This screen is about to display one of the most important lifetimes that came *after* your experience by the water. Just relax and allow the screen to become filled with a picture, a scene, the symbol of a culture, or whatever image will bring this period in history to mind. [Pause.]

Look around at this place. What do you see, feel, or just somehow know? Let the memories come forward and make a mental note of your experience . . . [Pause.] Where are you and what were you doing in that incarnation? [Pause.] What talents or abilities did you bring to that lifetime? [Pause.] Did you accomplish as a soul what you hoped to accomplish? Was anything left undone? [Pause.] If you can, imagine what your greatest strengths and weaknesses may have been at this period in history? [Pause.] Is there a picture or an image that can remind you of this lifetime? [Pause.] Are there any symbols that represent the strengths you came in with? [Pause.] Are there any symbols that represent the weaknesses you hoped to overcome? [Pause.] What images correspond to the level of learning or consciousness you achieved at that period in history? [Pause.] What do you bring from this experience into your present incarnation? [Pause.]

Next in your imagination, I want you to recall another important lifetime that came even later—a lifetime that had important experiences with other people. Try to visualize other people who were important to your soul journey standing before you. [Pause.] What do these people look like and what are they wearing? [Pause.] How were you involved with these individuals and what was the purpose of your incarnation at that time? [Pause.] What strengths or weaknesses did you bring to that life? [Pause.] What pictures or symbols might best remind you of this lifetime, your abilities, your shortcomings, and what you actually accomplished at that time? [Pause.] What is it about this incarnation that is most memorable to you in the present? [Pause.][4]

Next, in your imagination, I want you to think about your present life and some of your most memorable experiences in the present. [Pause.] For example, what are some of your most memorable experiences as a child? [Pause.] Who are the people you remember most and what did they teach you about your own strengths and weaknesses? [Pause.] As a child, can you remember what you wanted to be when you grew up? [Pause.] What cultures, historical periods, or major world events from the past were you most drawn to? [Pause.] Are there any symbols or images that can correspond to your memories, talents, or experiences as a child? [Pause.] Is there anything about yourself that you would like to change in terms of your own growth and development? [Pause.]

Finally, in your imagination, I want you to see a picture or a symbol, or a series of symbols that for you can represent the greatest spiritual attainment that you can imagine. [Pause.] In other words, what pictures might represent soul development and mastery for you at this time? [Pause.] What symbol is the most inspirational in helping you to remember your soul's ultimate goal? [Pause.]

Now in your imagination, I want you to imagine yourself sitting in your chair (or lying down) in *this present place, this present time, right now.* As you come back to your waking awareness, totally centered in the present, bring with you only those memories that are important, positive, and helpful. Other information you can release or forget. Imagine yourself firmly grounded in the present. Imagine yourself fully conscious, clearheaded, feeling fine, and aware of who you are right now.

OK, you can take another deep breath and open your eyes, feeling clearheaded, refreshed, and perfectly normal.

Note: You may wish to begin working on your aura chart while these images and memories are still fresh in your mind.

---

[4]Note: Depending on how many incarnations you hope to recall, you may wish to repeat one of the above paragraphs designed to bring past-life memories to your present day awareness, or you might wish instead to create additional memory-prompting paragraphs of your own.

CREATING YOUR OWN AURA CHART

After reflecting upon the above questions, ideas, and images, you may wish to draw or cut out some of the things that you saw or simply pull together some symbols and pictures. Remember, whatever you choose should be helpful in calling to mind the most important things and past-life memories that you would like to remember each time you look at your aura chart. As an example, let's imagine that an individual just completed the "A Journey into Your Imagination" reverie with the following results:

To begin with, perhaps an angel at the bottom of the chart reminds that person of the soul's spiritual beginnings.

Next, during the imaginative reverie let's say that an Egyptian lifetime was brought to mind as one of the soul's earliest memories. For that reason the first incarnation at the bottom of the chart corresponds to a lifetime in Egypt. Let's imagine that some of the strongest qualities that the soul came in with at that time corresponded to the positive traits associated with the astrological sign for Aquarius: idealism and humanitarianism. Perhaps during that same incarnation, the soul encountered individuals from all walks of life and cultural backgrounds, enabling the person to broaden his or her vision even further in the process—the sign of Jupiter might symbolize this effectively.

Moving further up the chart, perhaps the next incarnation seen was as a Mayan Indian with a family. Some of the experiences associated with the talents and abilities of the soul were associated with mysticism and the mysterious. For that reason, the symbol of Neptune appears on the left. A heart appears on the right because the individual achieved love of family during that same period. (Depending on the person's knowledge of symbolism, he or she might have just as easily placed the symbol for the astrological sign of Cancer on the right to symbolize the same thing.)

One of the most recent incarnations recalled by the individual is pictured near the top. A boat and the pilgrims suggest a search for a new life and a New World. Pisces on the left can be suggestive of spirituality. (It can also correspond with being prone to impractical ideas, such as moving to the other side of the world.) Taurus on the right can correspond to the determination and endurance that the pilgrims had to display in order to achieve their dreams in a new land. Perhaps the person recognizes this streak of bravery and willingness to take chances as an integral part of her or his individuality in the present.

Finally, let's imagine that the individual equates at-one-ment (or oneness with the divine) as the highest spiritual reality attainable in the present. For that reason, a picture of a meditator might be the appropriate image. However the individual decides to create her or his personal chart is up to that person, because the chart is not necessarily shared with anyone else. What is important is to pull together symbols and images that can encapsulate the soul memory, the individuality, and the ultimate attainment the person hopes to achieve.

Taking all of the above into consideration, the resulting aura chart might look something like the one at the end of this chapter.

The Edgar Cayce readings suggest that aura charts are physical reminders of the soul's spiritual journey. Through the use of pictures and symbols, charts can embody an inspirational glimpse of the soul's individuality. They provide a positive look at the soul's strengths as well as those personal shortcomings that may need to be transformed or overcome. This emphasis on the rationale for coming to know one's self and self's journey through time is perhaps explained in terms of what Cayce told a twenty-eight-year-old insurance clerk in 1939: "For, if individuals were as mindful of what they have been as they are of what they are to be, this would become a much more interesting as well as a purposeful experience..." (1968-1)

Because the awareness of the soul's individuality is influenced by a person's consciousness at any moment in time, these charts can be updated, redrawn, or revised whenever it is desirable to do so. In the Cayce files it also becomes apparent that individuals pass through a variety of experiences and encounters in life when different incarnations from the soul's past have greater relevance and others are not quite as important. Certainly, the soul's ultimate attainment can remain the same but the talents and resources drawn upon in the present as well as the challenges and lessons that seem to be facing the individual can change at any point in time.

An aura chart is essentially a physical rendering of pictures, symbols, and images that can assist you in better understanding who you really are while reminding you of what you ultimately hope to become. Creating and then working with an aura chart can be helpful for individuals interested in coming to terms with their strengths and weaknesses, their highest aspirations, their talents and abilities, and those experiences from the past that are having an important effect on the present. Using aura charts is one of the tools for working with personal symbolism that was recommended by the Edgar Cayce readings. It is a tool that can help facilitate personal understanding and self-awareness, soul development and personal transformation, and an overall understanding of an individual's soul purpose in life.

Possible Creation of Personal Aura Chart

Image 10
Archetypal Drawing for Edgar Cayce, drawn by Nancy Lansdale

Image 11
Aura Chart for Edgar Cayce, painted by Esther Wynne

Image 12
The Edgar Cayce Aura Chart, Oil on Canvas, 70" x 50",
1967-1969, artist: Ingo Swann

Image 13
Aura Chart for Mrs. [2390], painted by Esther Wynne

Image 14
Aura Chart for Mr. [533], painted by Esther Wynne

Image 15
Aura Chart for Gertrude Cayce, painted by Esther Wynne

Image 16
Aura Chart for Mr. [462], painted by Esther Wynne

Part Three: The Revelation

Then he flew to the water, and swam towards the beautiful swans. The moment they espied the stranger, they rushed to meet him with outstretched wings.

"Kill me," said the poor bird; and he bent his head down to the surface of the water, and awaited death.

But what did he see in the clear stream below? His own image; no longer a dark, gray bird, ugly and disagreeable to look at, but a graceful and beautiful swan. To be born in a duck's nest, in a farmyard, is of no consequence to a bird, if it is hatched from a swan's egg. He now felt glad at having suffered sorrow and trouble, because it enabled him to enjoy so much better all the pleasure and happiness around him; for the great swans swam round the newcomer, and stroked his neck with their beaks, as a welcome.

Into the garden presently came some little children, and threw bread and cake into the water.

"See," cried the youngest, "there is a new one;" and the rest were delighted, and ran to their father and mother, dancing and clapping their hands, and shouting joyously, "There is another swan come; a new one has arrived."

Then they threw more bread and cake into the water, and said, "The new one is the most beautiful of all; he is so young and pretty." And the old swans bowed their heads before him.

Then he felt quite ashamed, and hid his head under his wing; for he did not know what to do, he was so happy, and yet not at all proud. He had been persecuted and despised for his ugliness, and now he heard them say he was the most beautiful of all the birds. Even the elder-tree bent down its bows into the water before him, and the sun shone warm and bright. Then he rustled his feathers, curved his slender neck, and cried joyfully, from the depths of his heart, "I never dreamed of such happiness as this, while I was an ugly duckling."

Excerpt from *The Ugly Duckling*
Hans Christian Andersen, 1844

7

The Revelation as a Symbolic Journey in Personal Consciousness

One of the areas of symbolism most examined by Edgar Cayce and his colleagues that at the same time continues to be most overlooked by the contemporary world is the readings' information on the Book of Revelation. Perhaps one reason is because the symbolism and imagery that appears within the last book of the New Testament seems difficult to understand at best and possibly frightening to consider at worst. Another possibility is that the text of Revelation has often been viewed as a book of prophecy mainly applicable to some future generation. However, the insights available from the Cayce readings completely transform the most commonly accepted ideas regarding what the book is all about. From Cayce's perspective the Book of Revelation is not about prophetic doom; instead the imagery and symbolism actually hold clues to the evolution of human consciousness—a universal pattern of growth and transformation available to all of humankind. In this regard, the Revelation becomes personally relevant for every individual, regardless of creed, race, or period of existence in human history.

Although it is now contested among biblical scholars, early tradition held that John the Beloved Apostle wrote the Revelation or Book of the Apocalypse during his exile to the penal island of Patmos, where he had been sent as punishment for having preached Christianity. Thought to be one of the oldest texts of the New Testament, most scholars believe that the Revelation was written somewhere between 54 and 96 AD and came as a result of a visionary experience had by John during a period of intense prayer and meditation.

For literally hundreds of years, countless students of the Bible have interpreted John's Revelation to be a prophetic vision of horrific events that will eventually face the entire planet. These events are thought to include a global battle between the forces of good and evil and the eventual reign of an Antichrist that will subject all of humankind to his control. With this interpretation in mind, throughout history people have often attempted to surmise the identity of this "Antichrist," perhaps as a means of being forewarned. In fact, even a casual search of the Internet will result in dozens of possible identities for this demonic character that include such personalities as: Hitler, Napoleon, the emperor Charlemagne, Osama bin Laden, the emperor Nero, Saddam Hussein, Stalin, Mussolini, and even the Pope.

Many individuals who have accepted an interpretation of John's experience along the lines of global cataclysm might be surprised to learn that the word "antichrist" does not even appear in the Book of Revelation. In fact, in the entire Bible the word antichrist appears only in the epistles of John and seems to suggest that an antichrist is simply an individual who denies the identity of Jesus as the Christ—the long-awaited Messiah (see especially 1 John 2:22 and 1 John 4:3). In other words, rather than being some kind of a worldwide nemesis, this type of individual would simply be against or "anti-Christ."

The traditional prophetic approach has also made much of the various beasts that appear in the Revelation imagery. The most fearsome seems to be the two beasts in Revelation 13. One of these beasts is described as having seven heads and ten horns and possessing the image of a leopard, the feet of a bear, and the mouth of a lion (Revelation 13:1-2). But if this is John's prophetic vision, why did the prophet Daniel have a dream more than four hundred years earlier in which similar animal characteristics appeared to him? In Daniel's dream, four beasts emerge and include the leopard, the bear, and the lion, along with an unnamed monster (Daniel 7:4-7).

In addition, just as Daniel saw four beasts, the image of four beasts also makes an appearance in Revelation 4:7. However, in this instance the beasts are described as a lion, a man, a calf, and an eagle. The traditional approach to Revelation suggests that for some, these beasts are symbolic representations of the creatures of the earth. Humankind corresponds to the man, the eagle represents the birds of the air, the lion is associated with the creatures of the wild, and the calf corresponds to domesticated and friendly creatures. Others suggest that these beasts represent the powers that often sway humankind from its rightful devotion to God, such as government, religion, the devil, business, and so forth.

Rather than simply accepting this as a portion of some prophetic vision of the future, however, we might wish to consider why the prophet Ezekiel saw a vision of four identical beasts approximately five hundred years earlier: a man, a lion, an ox, and an eagle (Ezekiel 1:10). It is also interesting to note that the creature of the lion seen in Daniel's dream possessed the wings of an eagle and the feet of a man (Daniel 7:4), incorporating three of the four animal characteristics seen in both Revelation and in Ezekiel's vision.

In addition to these similarities, the early Church adopted the images of an eagle, a lion, a man, and an ox to represent the four writers of the Gospels who had been divinely inspired by God. According to Church tradition, the eagle corresponds to John, the lion is associated with Mark, the man is symbolic of Matthew, and the ox represents Luke. Even today, many churches throughout the world contain these symbolic representations of the four evangelists somewhere within the church, on the walls, decorating the internal columns, or even carved upon the building's façade.

Since the images of these four creatures can all be traced to an altered state of awareness, is it possible that these experiences might suggest something about the nature of human consciousness? In other words, since each of the experiences that resulted in the perception of these four creatures can be connected to a vision, a dream, a meditative experience, or divine inspiration, is there another interpretation that focuses not simply on prophecy but rather on the nature of humankind? In fact, it is this very approach in which the Revelation is seen as a means of better understanding the human condition that is explored by a wealth of insights contained in the Edgar Cayce information.

Cayce's unique approach to studying the Book of Revelation can be traced to January 1930 when parents of a twenty-year-old woman checked their daughter into the Edgar Cayce Hospital for treatment of a condition that they described as "nervous irritability." For ten years the couple had sought a variety of medical treatments for the young woman but the condition persisted. The girl's symptoms included nervousness and an uncontrollable twitching of her face, hands, and limbs. She also possessed an irritable disposition and was unable to control her volatile emotions even in public. The girl's mother was at her wit's end and admitted, "I had reached what seemed to be the limit of my endurance and seriously considered any step that would mean relief." (2501-11 Reports)

Cayce's suggested treatments for this patient included osteopathy, medical injections, a change in diet, and energy work—all designed to bring balance to the girl's physical body and glandular systems. During a follow-up reading in which both the mother and attending physician were present, Cayce gave some surprising advice. He suggested that it would be beneficial for the doctor in charge of the case to read the Book of Revelation and to try and understand the Revelation especially in relationship to what was occurring within the body and mind of his twenty-year-old patient.[5]

Although there is no record as to whether or not the doctor ever followed through on the suggestion, three weeks later during the course of a follow-up reading (2501-7), the question was asked as to

---

[5]Note: Because of her stay in the hospital, the young woman was healed of her condition and would eventually lead a happy and healthy life as the mother of three children.

why it had been suggested to study the Revelation in connection with the body. Cayce's reply suggested that not only did the Revelation provide an illustration of what transpired within an individual as he or she evolved in consciousness but that this illustration showed the activity of the spiritual centers of the body (corresponding to the body's endocrine centers). Cayce added that anyone could understand this connection simply by comparing the Revelation with the anatomical structures of the body. Apparently, the young woman's problem was traceable to an incoordination of the activity of her endocrine glands. As an aside, the reading also pointed out that there was a symbolic connection between the Old Testament's detailed depiction of the temple and the fact that the body was actually the temple or the place where the spirit and the physical could meet.

Years later, the readings advised a fifty-five-year-old chiropractor that if he really wanted to understand himself and others he needed to read the Book of Revelation "with the idea of the body as the interpretation." (4083-1) Similar advice was given to a twenty-eight-year-old student working toward his Ph.D. in art and history who asked during the course of a reading what passages of the Bible he should study. Edgar Cayce's recommendations included the Book of Revelation, calling it "the revelation of self." The reading added:

> And in the Revelation study as this: Know, as there is given each emblem, each condition, it is representing or presenting to self a study of thine own body, with *all* of its emotions, all of its faculties. All of its physical centers represent experiences through which thine own mental and spiritual and physical being pass. For it is indeed the revelation of self.   1173-8

Another interesting correlation had come as early as 1926 when Cayce informed a thirty-year-old Jewish stockbroker that if he really wanted to understand the divine within, he needed to study the book *Gray's Anatomy* (900-190). Similar advice was given to a forty-one-year-old housewife in 1931, who was told that she could understand the connection between the human body and metaphysics simply by comparing and contrasting the Book of Revelation with *Gray's Anatomy* (264-15). During a follow-up reading, Cayce told the same woman that the Book of Revelation provided an understanding of what transpired within an individual "when the vibrations are raised within the body through meditation, or through that of fasting and prayer." (264-19) Drawing upon these suggestions connecting the physical body, consciousness growth and attunement, and the symbolism of Revelation, over a period of ten years (1933-1943) members of a prayer group calling themselves the "Glad Helpers" explored this understanding of the Book of Revelation with Edgar Cayce in greater detail.

Originally founded in 1931, the Glad Helpers prayer group consisted of individuals interested in prayer, meditation, and spiritual healing. Generally composed of between seven and fourteen individuals, this small group's primary desire was to become a healing prayer group that could assist others through the power of prayer. In addition to their work with prayer and spiritual healing, the group was encouraged to make an exhaustive study of the endocrine system and the Book of Revelation. The rationale suggested by the readings was that such a study was essential to truly understanding the points of contact between the divine/spirit and the physical structures of the body.

During the group's first reading about the Revelation, Cayce told those present that it was important to remember that the Revelation had occurred to the Apostle John during his exile on the Isle of Patmos after the death of Jesus. Apparently John had been in prayer and meditation, seeking insights as to how he might best carry on his work. Cayce suggested that John's encounter was a visionary experience of the internal struggles that take place within an individual as consciousness and soul development takes place. Rather than simply being an experience applicable only to John, the readings contend that the symbolism and imagery was relevant for every individual:

> For the visions, the experiences, the names, the churches, the places, the dragons, the cities, all are but emblems of those forces that may war within the individual in its journey through the material, or from the entering into the material manifestation to the entering into the glory, or

> the awakening in the spirit, in the inter-between, in the
> borderland, in the shadow.   281-16

With this in mind, the Cayce information suggests that one way to explore the Book of Revelation is one of archetypal or universal symbolism. Through a series of images and pictures, the Revelation portrays a sequential process that corresponds to the awakening of the higher self. It depicts the internal struggles that occur within each individual as spiritual development takes place and the basic lower nature of humankind evolves to its higher spiritual nature. In simplest terms, the Revelation is essentially a handbook for the sequential evolution of human consciousness as individuals reawaken to their connection to the divine.

The Cayce approach to the Revelation sees the imagery of the text as first and foremost a symbolic look at what occurs within individuals as attunement takes place. Therefore, rather than looking for external events, people, or activities to identify with the symbols, the Cayce readings suggest looking instead for a corresponding process or structure within the physical body. As one example, Cayce suggested that the seven candlesticks within the first chapter of the Revelation refer not to the menorah of the Old Testament temple but rather to the seven endocrine centers within the physical body. These seven centers serve as points of contact between the spiritual chakras and the physical body and are identified with the following glandular systems: the gonads, the cells of Leydig (sometimes referred to as the lyden), the adrenals, the thymus, the thyroid, the pineal, and the pituitary. With this in mind, the seven spirits that are before the throne are these points of contact with the divine (Revelation 1:4). These same glands also correspond to the seven churches. Because of Cayce's ongoing correlation between the body and the symbolism of John's vision, it becomes clear why the readings recommended a comparative study between the Book of Revelation and *Gray's Anatomy.*

The endocrine centers are physical glands that correspond—according to Cayce—with the spiritual centers or chakras; they are not identical structures. For example, an individual could have an operation that physically removed the adrenals, and he or she would still possess the spiritual chakra corresponding to that level. The term "chakra" is actually a Sanskrit word meaning "wheel" because of the way in which the energy associated with the spiritual centers appear to spin in place. This becomes especially relevant when it is considered that the faces of the four beasts seen by Ezekiel in the Old Testament were identified with four wheels (Ezekiel 1:15-17). This suggests that Ezekiel witnessed the activity of his own spiritual centers being awakened, stimulating the archetypal imagery associated with the four lower centers.

Building upon the insights obtained by the Glad Helpers prayer group, for nearly thirty years Cayce scholar Herbert Bruce Puryear, Ph.D., made a careful study of the Edgar Cayce information on the Revelation. An author, psychologist, and noted biblical student, Puryear eventually outlined a seven-step sequence as a means of better understanding this evolutionary process of attunement and developing consciousness. Believing that it is perhaps more important to read and experience the Revelation rather than simply attempting to interpret the symbolism, Dr. Puryear suggested that one read it aloud and "think of it as experiencing music rather than reading information." (Puryear, *Covenant,* Lesson XXII) In this manner, the archetypal imagery of John's Revelation has the capability of awakening an internal response. Just like uplifting music, it can cause a powerful quickening within the consciousness of the individual simply by hearing a recitation of the text. Although there is some overlap between the sequences and the various chapters, Puryear's seven-step process essentially divides the twenty-two chapters of Revelation as follows[6]:

Revelation Chapters	Sequence	Activity within the Individual
Chapters 1-4	Addressing the Seven Churches	Self-Evaluation
Chapters 5-8	Opening the Seven-Sealed Book	Opening of the Seven Centers
Chapters 8-11	Sounding the Seven Trumpets	Personal Purification

Revelation Chapters	Sequence	Activity within the Individual
Chapters 12-14	The Appearance of Seven Personages Ideal	Establishment of the Higher Self as the
Chapters 15-16	Seven Angels with Seven Vials	Meeting the Karmic Memory of the Seven Centers
Chapters 17-20	The Fall of Babylon	Overthrowing the Dominion of the Lower Self
Chapters 21-22	A New Heaven and a Earth	Ascendancy of the New Higher Self

[6]This chart is essentially a combination of Puryear's "Covenant lessons XXII-XXIII," dealing with the Revelation, and a public lecture given in 1983: "The Revelation: Keys to Christian Mysticism."

As a means of better understanding the archetypal symbolism, the information obtained by the Glad Helpers prayer group, Puryear's sequential process, and how this information relates to the individual, what follows is an exploration of some of this material in greater detail:

REVELATION 1-4: ADDRESSING THE SEVEN CHURCHES—SELF-EVALUATION

In this first sequence John is in meditation ("in the spirit") and turns to see seven golden candlesticks, which represent the seven endocrine centers or chakras. In the midst of these candlesticks, he sees the Son of Man who tells him to write what he is about to witness. This suggests that the activity of the universal Christ presence is important for John's attunement to continue. This Being holds seven stars in his right hand and places this hand upon John, suggesting that these seven cen-

ters are somehow instrumental in establishing the point of contact between the body and the spirit. John is then told to begin writing letters
to the seven churches of Asia Minor.

During the process of meditation, the energy of attunement that has
been called by some the kundalini begins to rise through the seven
spiritual centers. As this occurs, various images and symbols can come
to mind, corresponding to the energy passing through each of the various centers. From Cayce's perspective, it was not by chance that both
Ezekiel in the Old Testament and John in the Revelation witnessed the
images of a calf (or ox), a man, a lion, and an eagle. In fact, each of
these symbols correspond to the four lower centers in the body (the
gonads, the cells of Leydig, the adrenals, and the thymus, respectively). Therefore, as each individual meditated, the archetypal symbol for each center was awakened and became an accompanying vision
as the energy of the kundalini began to rise and pass through it.

John's act of writing a letter to the seven churches within the first
four chapters is actually symbolic of the need for all individuals to
take a personal assessment of the self's qualities and faults related to
each of these motivational centers. In the language of the readings:
"Then, seek to know what self is lacking, even as given in the first
four chapters . . . Are ye cold? Are ye hot? Have ye been negligent of
the knowledge that is thine? Are ye stiff-necked? Are ye adulterous in
thought, in act, in the very glories that are thine?" (281-16) This same
idea of the need to undergo a self-evaluation before proceeding with
personal attunement is found elsewhere in the New Testament when
Jesus cautions about the importance of becoming reconciled with any
individual with whom there is a problem before entering into the
temple (Mark 5:23-24).

The church of Ephesus relates to the gonad center. During this
evaluation process, John recognizes that the strength of his own motivational center has been patience; however, a weakness at this level is
that this center has left its first love. In Cayce's cosmology, the soul
was created to become a companion and co-creator with God. The
Bible states, "Thou shalt love the Lord thy God with all thy heart, and
with all thy soul, and with all thy mind, and with all thy strength,"
(Mark 12:30) and, "Thou shalt have no other Gods before me." (Exo-

dus 20:3) Therefore, the act of leaving the first love refers to setting the love of God (the first love) aside in preference for other things.

As the energy continues to rise and touches upon the cells of Leydig center, John's letter to the church of Smyrna symbolizes the evaluation that occurs at this level. The strength of this center is its ability to deal with tribulation (suffering). The corresponding weakness is associated with insincerity ("the blasphemy of them which say they are Jews, and are not").

The church of Pergamos is symbolic of the third center, which is the adrenals. The virtue at this level corresponds to remaining steadfast in faith. The fault is related to the act of casting stumbling blocks before others (e.g., creating doubt or confusion in the minds of others).

While exploring this segment of John's revelation, the Glad Helpers prayer group inquired about the meaning of Revelation 2:17 and the statement that whoever overcame would receive hidden manna, a white stone, and a new name. Cayce stated each soul has a unique and individual name that he or she was given by God. With this in mind, receiving a new name is actually symbolic of achieving that selfhood that had been intended by the Creator—of fulfilling one's intended mission in life. The hidden manna correlates to the spiritual sustenance and understanding that becomes available to any that remain steadfast in faith. The white stone represents the purity that results for those who undergo hardship and endure (281-31).

The fourth center is the thymus and it is represented by the church of Thyatira. The corresponding strength is charity (love) and the associated fault is fornication (e.g., squandering its energy on selfishness or less than the highest good, whether it's related to sex for self-gratification or to doing that which it knows is not for the greatest good).

At this level the individual is told that he or she will receive the morning star. The morning star is Venus, which is the planet symbolic of love. This suggests that the capacity for divine love becomes a part of the individual who cultivates the virtue of this center.

The thyroid is symbolized by the church of Sardis, identified with the fifth center. The strength is its ability to remain steadfast in seeking spiritual ideals ("not defiled their garments"); however, its weakness is imperfection ("I have not found thy works perfect").

The sixth center is the pineal and it corresponds to the sixth church, which is Philadelphia. The virtue at this level is "an open door" that is not dependent upon the activities of any human. In other words, at this level the connection to spirit has remained unaffected by the individual. For that reason, there is not a fault or weakness associated with John's vision at this level—the motivational center has remained true to its purpose.

The seventh and final church is Laodicea, corresponding to the pituitary. The weakness is stated as being "neither cold nor hot" or "lukewarm." The lack of an identified virtue at this level suggests that because of the lukewarm nature of this motivational center the virtue for John has yet to be activated.

The ultimate promise of John's revelation is revealed to all those who overcome the seventh and final level. Revelation 3:21 states, "To him that overcometh will I grant to sit with me in my throne, even as I also overcame, and am set down with my Father in his throne." Repeatedly the Cayce readings suggest that Jesus exemplified the universal Christ Consciousness—a pattern of awareness of the soul's true connection to the divine. Each individual was created to ultimately become a companion with the divine in the same manner that was shown by Jesus. With this in mind, in 1938 a twenty-three-year-old sailor was told:

> The purpose for the entrance of each soul into a material experience is for the development that it, the soul, may be a companion with the Creative Forces. For that purpose this entity, this soul—as all others—came into being; to be a companion with the Creator.   1641-1

The assessment that is done at the level of each of the seven centers—symbolized by John's letters to the churches—is essentially an evaluation process in which the individual is asked to take stock of self's uses of these motivational energies, both negatively and positively. Following this same principle, the late Hugh Lynn Cayce, eldest son of Edgar Cayce, created a personal evaluation chart in his book *Faces of Fear* to explore some of these same potential uses of the creative energy associated with each of the seven centers. An adaptation of Hugh Lynn's chart is as follows:

Positive Potential Uses of the Energies Associated with the Centers:

Center	Potential Qualities and Strengths			
Gonads	Helpful	Protective	Serves Others	Meditates
Cells of Leydig	Resolute	Gentle	Balanced Male/Female Energies	Merciful
Adrenals	Seeks Peace with Others	Persistent	Faithful	Controls Temper
Thymus	Loving Others Before Self	Generous	Sympathetic	Friendly
Thyroid	Cooperative	Makes Wise Choices	Stands by Ideals	Open to Suggestions
Pineal	Possesses a Seeking Attitude	Knows Self	Reasonable	Aware of the Oneness of the Divine
Pituitary	Gives God Credit	Inspirational	Humble	Encourages Others

Negative Potential Uses of the Energies Associated with the Centers:

Center	Potential Faults and Weaknesses			
Gonads	Self-Indulgent	Lazy	Abusive	Neglects Spiritual Things
Cells of Leydig	Doubting	Irresponsible	Imbalance of Male/Female Energies	Inflexible
Adrenals	Overly Protective of Self	Discouraged	Domineering	Angry
Thymus	Loving Self	Selfish	Self-pity	Withdrawn
Thyroid	Willful	Makes Irresponsible Decisions	Does not Apply Spiritual Ideals	Indecisive
Pineal	Narrow-minded	Does Not Know Self	Unreasonable	Unaware or Indifferent to Oneness
Pituitary	Self-righteous	Indifferent	Arrogant	Deflates Others

(Cayce, *Faces,* pgs. 120-121)

After this period of self-evaluation in which the individual takes account of the faults and virtues of the major motivational potentials within self, the next image within the Revelation text is of a throne surrounded by twenty-four elders and four beasts. Remembering that the readings' approach is to associate the symbolism with a corresponding activity or structure within the body, Cayce identified the twenty-four elders as the twenty-four cranial nerves within the head, especially as they relate to the five senses. According to *Gray's Anatomy*, there are essentially twelve pairs of nerves (corresponding to the image of twenty-four) that are a part of the peripheral nervous system and are most associated with the activity of the five senses: sight, hearing, taste, smell, and touch. (Gray, pgs. 903-905)

In addition to identifying the four beasts (calf, man, lion, and eagle) as being associated with the four lower centers (gonads, cells of Leydig, adrenals, and thymus, respectively), Cayce stated that the four beasts also correspond to the four basic natures of humankind. These basic natures or desires essentially embody the following motivations: self-sustenance (gonads), self-propagation (cells of Leydig), self-preservation (adrenals), and self-gratification (thymus).

The sea of glass that resides next to the four beasts can be associated with the stilled emotions during the process of meditation. The symbolism might also indicate the stilled energy of the kundalini.

In John's vision, the four beasts and the twenty-four elders all become subservient and begin worshipping the throne of God. This symbolism suggests that the four basic self-motivations as well as the five senses must become subservient, bringing their attention to this process of inner attunement. It is only after this occurs that John's revelation can continue.

REVELATION 5-8:
OPENING THE SEVEN-SEALED BOOK—
OPENING OF THE SEVEN CENTERS

In the second sequence, John's experience essentially entails witnessing the opening of the seven-sealed book and the accompanying visions. At the beginning of this sequence, John becomes aware that only the sacrificed Lamb (associated with the Christ) is worthy to open the book and to loosen the seals. The Cayce readings state that the book with the seven seals corresponds to the human body with its seven spiritual centers. Therefore, the imagery suggests that the spiritual centers are sealed in ordinary life and no one should attempt to open these centers without the awareness of the spirit of the universal Christ Consciousness. The readings warn, "Do not attempt to open any of the centers of the book until self has been tried in the balance of self's own conscious relationship to the Creative Forces and not found wanting . . . " (281-29) Once again, in order for the attunement to continue, the four beasts and the twenty-four elders must bow down and become subservient to the overall process. The lamb can also represent a gentle, obedient spirit.

As will perhaps be seen more clearly in Revelation 17:12 with the image of the beast with seven heads and ten horns, a horn can be symbolic of desire. Whatever the mind dwells upon can grow and become a larger portion of the individual's thought processes. Keeping this in mind, a horn growing out of a head is an appropriate symbol for the activity of desire. On the other hand, an eye is obviously symbolic of awareness. Therefore, the slain Lamb with seven horns and seven eyes that alone is worthy to open the book (Revelation 5:6) is suggestive of the universal Christ Consciousness that has sacrificed both its awareness and its desires in preference for the divine.

With the opening of the first seal, John sees a white horse and rider going forth and conquering. The opening of the second seal results in the appearance of a red horse and rider that goes out with a great sword. The third seal is opened and John sees a black horse, with a rider carrying a pair of balances in his hand. When the fourth seal is opened, a pale horse rides forth whose rider has power over death. Historically, these four horses have often been seen as the symbolic representations of the four plagues of Pestilence (disease), War, Famine, and Death, respectively (Jewish Encyclopedia, Vol. X, pg. 392). The Glad Helpers prayer group, however, received a different interpretation of this imagery.

From Cayce's perspective, these horses are symbolic representations of the hormonal secretions (messengers) that ride forth from each of the four lower centers during the attunement-purification process or, in the language of the readings, the "physical forces that ride forth to their expression." (281-30) For that reason, John's vision of four horses provides an amazing similarity with the four horses seen by the prophet Zechariah in the Old Testament (Zechariah 6:1-3). The white horse is associated with the hormonal secretions of the gonads. The black horse corresponds to the functioning of the cells of Leydig. The red horse represents the hormones at the adrenal level. Finally, the pale horse (referred to as being "grisled" in Zechariah's vision) corresponds to the hormonal secretions of the thymus.

According to *Gray's Anatomy*, the endocrine glands release specific hormones directly into the blood stream. Emulating the imagery of the four horsemen messengers riding out into the earth, Gray states, "the hormones are chemical messengers . . . [that] are carried by the blood stream to all parts of the body . . . " (Gray, pg. 1341) Therefore, the imagery of riding forth and causing death and destruction is associated not with some type of external warfare but rather with the process of cleansing, attunement, and balance that occurs within the physical body as these hormonal messengers are released into the bloodstream. In other words, all of the cells within the physical body must be brought into alignment and balance with their own highest state of functioning and attunement or else be destroyed in the process. Elsewhere, Cayce states that this process occurs because the physical systems "must be as one, they must be compatible, they must be coordinant, they must be in the relative relationships one to another." (281-32) Keeping this interpretation in mind, the "ten thousand times ten thousand, and thousands of thousands" (Revelation 5:11) obviously represents all of the cells of the human body.

The visions associated with the opening of the fifth, sixth, and seventh seals correspond to the opening of the higher three spiritual centers. The vision of souls that had been "slain for the word of God" during the opening of the fifth seal is associated with the release of hormones from the thyroid. The white robes given to these individuals symbolize the purification process that will eventually impact the entire body. The vision of the opening of the sixth seal and the resulting earthquake corresponds to the release of hormones at the level of the pineal. The resulting image is that the entire earth (symbolic of the body) is affected by the opening of the sixth seal. Finally, a short while later the seventh seal is opened, representing the activity of the pituitary. The accompanying vision is of "silence in heaven about the space of half an hour." The readings state that this final vision is also symbolic of the "silence" of meditation—the "*Silence* if ye would hear the Voice of thy Maker!" (281-29).

In her book, *Dopey's Path to Enlightenment,* Gladys T. McGarey, M.D., a founding board member and past president of the American Holistic Medical Association, describes the basic functioning related to each of the seven glands. A longtime student and spokesperson of the Edgar Cayce information, Dr. Gladys is well versed in the readings information on the Book of Revelation and its connection to the physical body. Her summary of the basic activity of the glands is essentially as follows:

- The gonads (first center; corresponding to the testes in the male and the ovaries in the female) produces various sex hormones and is also responsible for the production of eggs in the female and sperm in the male.
- The cells of Leydig (second center) are responsible for the production of hormones that differentiate the male and female qualities. [Note: The Cayce readings repeatedly suggest that the second center is the "seat of the soul" and that there is also an important spiritual interrelationship between the functioning of the second and sixth centers.]
- The adrenals (third center) are associated with energy and power, producing the hormones adrenaline and cortisone, among others.
- The thymus (fourth center) is the master gland of the lower four centers. Its hormones are most concerned with the functioning of the immune system.
- The thyroid (fifth center) is concerned with the way the body metabolizes food and produces energy.
- The pineal (sixth center) produces melatonin, which is affected

by light, and hormones that have an affect on the body's cycles. It also influences day-night cycles. [Note: Cayce repeatedly states that the pineal gland in the brain is directly connected to the cells of Leydig. This direct link can be associated with personal spiritual experiences and even enlightenment.]

- The pituitary (seventh center) is known as the master gland as its functioning and hormones control all of the other glands of the body. (McGarey, pgs. 3-5)

Just after the opening of the sixth seal and just prior to the opening of the seventh, John witnesses a vision of four angels standing at the four corners of the earth holding back the wind (Revelation 7:1). When the Glad Helpers prayer group asked for an interpretation of this symbolism, Cayce replied that it was symbolic of putting on hold the four forces or influences that affect humankind (281-29). Cayce described those forces as environment, heredity, mental influences, and spiritual influences. From the readings' perspective, these mental influences also include "innate mental urges" that are associated with various planes of consciousness that have been a portion of the soul's learning agenda (1895-1). The spiritual influences also include talents, weaknesses, and traits that are due to each soul's past-life influences.

The four influences are put on hold as a means of enabling the 144,000 which have been sealed (Revelation 7:4) to have an influence upon the rest of the body. During this period of relative calm, the new pattern of the higher self or the spiritual ideal can be established. This process is described in the Revelation text as "we have sealed the servants of our God in their foreheads." (Revelation 7:3)

The readings correlate the 144,000 with the "spiritualized" cells of each of the twelve major tribes (structures) of the body. In other words, these are the cells that are in perfect attunement with the body's proper functioning and, according to Cayce, can have a vibratory influence upon the rest of the body (281-30). The hormonal secretions that occur with the opening of the seals is the process that apparently awakens their activity.

After studying the readings and attempting to correlate the twelve tribes with the twelve major divisions of the physical body, members of the Glad Helpers prayer group originally listed the twelve bodily systems to include such things as the organs, glands, nerves, circulation, and so forth (281-63). Drawing instead upon the organization of subject matter contained in *Gray's Anatomy*, Dr. Herbert Bruce Puryear eventually updated the listing of twelve major bodily systems to be categorized as follows:

1. Osteology (the bones)
2. Joints and Ligaments
3. Muscles and Fasciae (connective tissue)
4. Circulatory System (heart, arteries, and veins)
5. Lymphatic System
6. Nervous System (central and peripheral)
7. Organs of the Senses
8. Integument (the skin)
9. Respiratory System
10. Digestive System
11. Urogenital System (urinary and reproductive organs)
12. Endocrine Glands

(Puryear, "Christian Mysticism")

After the 144,000 are sealed, there appears "a great multitude" (Revelation 7:9), once again corresponding to the rest of the cells of the body. In John's vision this multitude begins to worship God. This suggests that the awakening of these perfectly functioning cells can bring the rest of the body into attunement, or what the Glad Helpers prayer group described as "the rest of the cellular structure in the process of spiritualization." (281-29)

REVELATION 8-11: SOUNDING THE SEVEN TRUMPETS—PERSONAL PURIFICATION

The third sequence continues the process of attunement and personal purification, especially as it relates to each of the seven spiritual centers. During this segment, John sees seven angels sounding seven trumpets and witnesses the accompanying visions. Actually, in the imagery the first six angels sound their trumpets, each resulting in a corresponding vision. At that point, the four angels are finally allowed to release their hold upon the winds (the four forces/influences that affect humankind). John is then told that he must "prophesy again before many peoples" (Revelation 10:11) and he is given a reed with which to measure the temple of God. Afterwards, the seventh angel sounds the seventh trumpet, resulting in all the kingdoms of the earth becoming spiritualized and the twenty-four elders bowing down once again.

The readings suggest that the sounding of the seven trumpets specifically relates to the body's experience during physical purification after the opening of the seven seals. Before the sounding of the trumpets begins, however, an angel waves a golden censer (an ornamental container that holds incense) and causes the smoke from the incense to rise before the throne of God. When the Glad Helpers prayer group inquired about this imagery, they were told that the rising incense symbolized the acts of "good" that also rise before the throne of God. These acts include being "good, gentle, patient, merciful, [and] longsuffering." (281-30)

Apparently, just as the scent of incense can affect and influence an individual, these positive activities can have an ongoing influence upon the individual performing them. In other words, they can serve as a kind of internal "quickener" for anyone seeking to become in attunement with God. In addition to serving as a quickening influence upon the spiritualized forces of the body, this process also causes the unspiritualized and rebellious forces within the body to come to the individual's awareness. This is indicated by the angel throwing the censer into the earth (symbolic of the body) and John witnessing the unsettling experience as encompassing "voices, and thunderings, and lightnings, and an earthquake." (Revelation 8:5)

The sounding of the first four trumpets and the resulting visions is essentially the purification process that occurs within the first four centers—the gonads, the cells of Leydig, the adrenals, and the thymus. Cayce stated that fire could be seen as a purifying influence, just as hail (as the crystallization of water) could be a purifying influence.

In discussing this portion of the Revelation, the readings state: " . . . so all of these then represent those as figuratively of that as may be purified . . . and conquered and used for the development . . . and the oneness of the individual's purposes and desires." (281-31)

The original prayer group eventually realized that there was a symbolic connection between the four elements and the four lower spiritual centers, as follows: air = thymus; fire = adrenals; water = cells of Leydig; and, earth = gonads. In a similar manner, it was eventually found that an archetypal connection between the seven spiritual centers and the colors of the rainbow, the centers and the musical notes of a scale, and even the centers and some of the planets of the solar system could be theorized, as well.

As these lower centers are purified, the resulting imagery uses the elements of the earth to portray such things as hail, fire, and flood coming as devastations upon the earth. Rather than attempting to correlate John's vision with prophecies of future events, the readings reminded the prayer group that their study of the Book of Revelation was a study of self: "Now ye are studying yourself! Do not confuse the interpretation with that outside of thyself . . . " (281-30)

In other words, John's visions following the sounding of the trumpets relate to the conflicts within each individual and the various influences that are constantly warring with one another until the process of purification and at-onement has completely taken place. When the Revelation imagery portrays portions of the earth being destroyed, it corresponds to those portions of the body that remain rebellious or are out of alignment becoming transformed by hormones, attunement, or the activity of the immune system. When the imagery portrays much of humankind being killed or destroyed, it corresponds to individual cells that are out of attunement being destroyed, absorbed, eliminated, or transformed, as well.

The purification process for the three higher centers is identified with the three woes. The first woe is associated with locusts, an army of horsemen represents the second woe, and the third woe corresponds to the wrath of God and His temple being opened in heaven. The locusts that are released from the bottomless pit by the sounding of the fifth trumpet are symbolic of the lower bodily forces, vibrations, and influences that continue to exist at this point in the attunement process. Because they are connected to the fifth trumpet and therefore the fifth center, they also relate to the rebelliousness of the will. As suggested by the Revelation text, these nonharmonious influences cannot affect those portions of the individual that are already in attunement but only those "which have not the seal of God in their foreheads." (Revelation 9:4) However, it is inevitable that these rebellious aspects of the individual will eventually be brought under control, as is symbolized by the various descriptions of destruction and annihilation. Interestingly enough, the Greek word "apollyon" that is associated with the king of the bottomless pit actually means destroyer, just as its Hebrew equivalent of "abaddon" means ruin or destruction (Barker, *Everyone*, pg. 13).

The Revelation next portrays the sixth trumpet being sounded and the four angels releasing their hold upon the wind. The Cayce readings state that it is at this point the individual may "begin again to make practical or applicable, mentally, spiritually, materially, with that which has been thus far attained." (281-32) In other words, the individual must now continue to apply and attune to her or his understanding even in the face of the reawakened influences of hereditary, environment, and mental and spiritual forces that had abated for a time.

The army of "two hundred thousand thousand" horsemen (Revelation 9:16), corresponding to the second woe, are the multitude of rebellious and destructive forces within the individual that continue to be incompatible with the attunement and purification processes. As a destroying influence they must annihilate themselves and the remaining cells that are inharmonious with the whole, symbolized by the third part of men that are killed. Recall that the readings suggest from this point onward the body's structures and cells "must be as one . . . they must be in the relative relationships one to another." (281-32) The importance of the oneness of all force is an important aspect of this sixth center. Many of the inharmonious forces that remain shall be removed or transformed by the activity of the earthquake (a symbol for the activity of the pineal) that occurs just prior to the sounding of the seventh and final trumpet.

After the sounding of the sixth trumpet, another mighty angel appears holding a little book, which John is told will be sweet in the mouth and bitter in the belly. John eats the book as he is instructed to do and hears that he must now "prophesy again before many peoples, and nations, and tongues, and kings." (Revelation 10:11)

The little book is symbolic of the book of knowledge that is assimilated into the individual (eating the book). This knowledge relates to finally understanding the threefold nature of the self in terms of the physical, the mental, and the spiritual forces, as well as self's relationship to the divine. Once this level has been attained, Cayce asks, "What will ye do with that knowledge?"

At this level of spiritual growth not only is the individual held accountable in the present for the knowledge that has been acquired but also the individual apparently must become an example to others over and over again. The act of prophesying again before many individuals is symbolic of the act of repeatedly applying (in many experiences, before many people, even in many lifetimes) the knowledge that has been attained. In the language of the readings, "in many experiences, in many ways, in many environs, in many lands." (281-32)

This clearly suggests that once this level of enlightenment is attained, the individual is required to utilize their spiritual awareness in subsequent lifetimes and periods in history—much as the Revelation suggests for John. Is it any wonder that the knowledge becomes sweet in the mouth (wonderful to attain) but bitter in the belly (challenging to accept and apply)? Keeping this in mind the same reading states, "It is very beautiful to look upon, very beautiful to be desired; but in the application of same at times bitter."

The imagery in the eleventh chapter of Revelation essentially deals with John being given a reed to measure the temple, the activity and presence of the two witnesses, the sounding of the seventh trumpet, and the coming of the third woe. Afterward the temple of God is opened in heaven.

During the Glad Helpers exploration of chapter eleven the prayer group was told by the readings that John actually recognized the meaning and interpretation of his Revelation experience as it was occurring (281-33). Rather than being confused by the imagery, John evidently recognized his experience as being similar to that of other initiates in their studies of ancient wisdom. When he was told to measure the temple with a reed, he was actually being instructed to decide how all-encompassing his understanding was going to be, thereby establishing a baseline against which he could measure himself. In other words, John was being asked to decide how universal his understanding of the love of God and the oneness of all humankind was going to be. Was it going to be limited to one denomination or was is going to include everyone? John is being asked to determine how large his "heaven" is going to be.

This process of determining and then measuring self's understanding is applicable to everyone: "Who will you put in your heaven? Ye of a denomination, ye of a certain creed, ye of a certain measurement . . . " Cayce reminded the prayer group, "With what measure ye mete it is measured to thee again." (281-32)

The reference to the Gentiles in Revelation 11:2 being outside of the temple is simply symbolic of those people that are beyond the bounds of the inclusiveness or the understanding that an individual at this level of spiritual attainment has chosen for herself or himself. This activity of measuring the breadth of one's personal understanding is also contained in the Old Testament in the experiences of both the prophets Ezekiel and Zechariah (Ezekiel 40 and Zechariah 2, respectively). Evidently, once a certain level of spiritual attainment has been reached, the individual is asked to determine how much of humankind he or she will be willing to serve. With all of this in mind, the prayer group was encouraged to stretch their understanding beyond that normally associated with their conscious minds, while being reminded that the power and force of an all-loving God was infinite.

The two witnesses (symbolized by the two olive trees as well as the two candlesticks) are actually two of the four influences that affect humankind. In this case, one of the witnesses is the mental urges that are associated with various planes of consciousness that have been a portion of the soul's learning agenda, and the other is the spiritual influences that are due to previous incarnations. Cayce also correlates these two witnesses with the subconscious and superconscious portions of the individual. Using this association, the images of the locales of Sodom and Egypt referred to in the Revelation's text have an interesting correlation. It suggests that as an individual continues to work with attunement and overcoming the rebellious aspects of the self associated with these two influences there can be a release from the bondage (Egypt) of the self and an overcoming or a meeting of the sin/error (Sodom) of selfishness.

The revival of these same witnesses is simply a reflection of a statement that Jesus had apparently made to the Apostles. According to Cayce, they had been told that if they held true to the path of spiritual development that He was trying to emulate, "then I will bring to thy remembrance *all things*—from the foundations of the world!" (281-33), which would encompass all personal soul memories, including lessons attained, personal experiences, and past lives. In other words, at this level the individual moves beyond simply the present self and deals with all of the soul memories, bringing them into attunement and overcoming the rebellious forces at these deeper levels as well.

Once those rebellious forces that would attempt to overrule the attunement and at-onement process are overcome (e.g., those which would destroy the earth are destroyed), the seventh trumpet is sounded and the temple of God is opened. This suggests that the face-to-face communion with the divine that in the Old Testament was limited to the high priest in the inner court of the temple (1 Kings 8:6, 2 Chronicles 5:7, etc.) is now available to the initiate that has attained to this level. Finally, the consciousness of the self may become attuned to the superconsciousness of the divine.

REVELATION 12-14: THE APPEARANCE OF SEVEN PERSONAGES—ESTABLISHMENT OF THE HIGHER SELF AS THE IDEAL

The fourth sequence deals primarily with the appearance and interaction of seven characters or personages. These characters and their order of appearance are as follows:

1) a woman clothed with the sun (Revelation 12:1)
2) a child, travailing in birth (Revelation 12:2)
3) a great red dragon (Revelation 12:3)

4) Michael, the archangel (Revelation 12:7)
5) a beast, rising out of the sea (Revelation 13:1)
6) a beast, coming out of the earth (Revelation 13:11)
7) a Lamb with 144,000 faithful (Revelation 14:1)

The woman (1) represents all of those experiences in the earth and materiality that have brought the individual to this point in time. The birth of the child (2) corresponds to the appearance or birth of a spiritual ideal. (It is also associated with the birth of the universal Christ Consciousness.) The red dragon (3) is symbolic of those rebellious forces within self that would attempt to destroy this higher ideal. Michael (4) represents those spiritual forces that would assist, guide, and protect the individual on his or her path toward enlightenment. The war in heaven between Michael and the red dragon is symbolic of the conflict that occurs between one's spiritual ideal and the material and selfish concerns that have become part of the individual's consciousness.

The symbolism of the red dragon (3) possessing seven heads and ten horns (Revelation 12:3) is identical to the beast rising out of the sea (5) with seven heads and ten horns (Revelation 13:1). In both cases the seven heads are associated with the rebellious nature of each of the seven centers, whereas the ten horns correspond to the conflicting desires within each of the five senses that continually war with one another. The imagery of the ten horns is also repeated in Revelation 17:12.

When the red dragon is cast from heaven into the earth, the spiritual forces appear to reign supreme. However, that supremacy is challenged by the rebirth of rebellious forces previously thought to have been overcome. For that reason, the first beast appears to have been mortally wounded but instead survives (Revelation 13:3). Remembering that the cells of Leydig are associated with water and the gonads are associated with the earth, the imagery of the two new beasts is suggestive of the rebelliousness of two of the lower centers reemerging.

The beast rising out of the sea (5) is associated with the cells of Leydig and the individual's motivation of self-propagation rising up in rebellion. Conversely, the beast coming up out of the earth (6) corresponds to the gonad center and the individual's motivation of self-sustenance feeling threatened by the establishment of a higher spiritual ideal. The animal imagery associated with each of these two beasts correlates with the animal natures and urges within each individual. Finally, the presence of the Lamb (7) and the 144,000 suggests that continual attunement and adherence to the spiritual ideal will enable those aspects within self that are in attunement and have been quickened to overcome this rebirth of the spirit of rebellion.

Returning to some of the remaining symbolism that is contained in this fourth sequence, the readings suggest that the woman being given "two wings of a great eagle" (Revelation 12:14) with which to flee is suggestive of an individual's flight from materiality and mental concerns. This rising above things of a lower nature enables the individual to transition toward things of a more spiritual nature. Since the eagle is also associated with the symbol of the thymus, the imagery may also suggest that this transition is facilitated by overcoming the fault that is associated with this fourth center (self-gratification) and cultivating the virtue associated with that same level (charity/love).

The flood coming out of the serpent's mouth to destroy the woman and child (Revelation 12:15) corresponds to the flood of emotions within self that rise up in rebellion, fearing the annihilation of self with the establishment of a spiritual ideal. The readings elaborate by stating, "know that there constantly arises within the sojourn in the life or in an experience in the earth the flood of emotions that make for doubt, fears, tribulation, disturbances, anxieties." (281-34)

Within this sequence, the prayer group asked for further explanation of those whose names are not written in the Book of Life (Revelation 13:8). Rather than suggesting that it has been foreordained that there are souls who will not achieve at-onement with God, Cayce reminded the group of the universality of God's love. In the language of the readings, "whosover *will* may take of the water of life." (281-34) Therefore, keeping in mind that the Revelation is actually the "revelation of self," the names not written in the Book of Life may actually refer to those aspects of self that are rebellious and can never be in keeping with the oneness of the divine. This would also correlate to the imperfect cellular structures that are out of attunement with the Whole.

When the Revelation text states "He that leadeth into captivity shall go into captivity; he that killeth with the sword must be killed with the sword" (Revelation 13:10), it is simply an amplification of the fact that all individuals draw to themselves the consequences of their actions. The same idea is contained in Galatians 6:7 and elsewhere: "Be not deceived; God is not mocked: for whatsoever a man soweth, that shall he also reap." In Cayce's cosmology, each individual must meet the entirety of personal karmic memory. In the next sequence, John's revelation will reveal how that memory can be met at the level of spiritual awareness rather than having to literally live it out in the earth.

In his *Covenant* lesson on the Revelation, Herb Puryear states that the second beast (6) is also connected to the false prophet stage of spiritual development. At this level an individual may be able to manifest spiritual gifts, such as healing and psychic ability (even miracles), but still remains spiritually immature (Puryear, *Covenant*, Lesson XXXIII). In spite of a heightened level of consciousness, the revelation of self is not yet complete. Rather than thinking he or she has arrived, the individual needs to continue on the path of soul growth and spiritual development, otherwise the individual may believe that spiritual mastery has been achieved and inadvertently get off the path. The readings also connect this false prophet stage with the statement Jesus made that many will do wonderful works in His name but He never knew them (Matthew 7:22-23). This is another way of suggesting that in spite of their ability to work wonders they have yet to arrive at the stage in which they are in full accord with the living spirit.

Throughout history, much has been made of the number of the beast being the number of a man, "six hundred three score and six" (666). This is because the Revelation text suggests that there will come a time when no one will be able to "buy or sell, save he that had the mark." (Revelation 13:17) The Cayce readings suggest that this is simply an indication of those activities, groups, organizations, and pursuits that lack the "consciousness of God." (281-34) With this in mind, putting self in accord with the mark of the beast suggests putting self's will and desires above that of the will of God. It can also indicate placing organizations, people, groups, or other influences above the will of God. The mark of the beast is symbolic of those man-made structures and desires guiding the individual's life rather than putting self in accord with the living spirit and true guidance.

Another way of approaching this same idea may be to recall that the purification process involves the attunement and alignment of the seven spiritual centers. Since the seventh center is associated with an awareness of the soul's connection to God, then being just short of that awareness could correspond to the number six. Repeatedly, the readings refer to the threefold nature of humankind (physical-mental-spiritual, as well as conscious-subconscious-superconscious). Lacking the awareness of God at each of these levels might therefore correspond to the number "666."

The readings repeatedly offer the only approach that can lead to attainment at the highest level. This is symbolized in Revelation by the Lamb being accompanied by the 144,000, "having his Father's name written in their foreheads." (Revelation 14:1) Paraphrasing the words of the Apostle Paul in Philippians 2:5, Cayce states the approach is best exemplified, "even as He, who thought it not robbery to make Himself equal with God, but *ever* recognized 'Of myself I can do nothing—only as the spirit of truth, of God, works in and through me may that be accomplished that is pleasing in His sight.'" (3051-2)

While examining the phrase "here is wisdom" (Revelation 13:18), Cayce expounded upon what that wisdom entailed to members of the prayer group:

> . . . there is only *one* God, *one* Christ, one faith . . . this is the whole law; to love the Lord thy God with all thy mind, thy body, thy soul; thy neighbor as thyself. This is the whole law. This is wisdom. This is knowledge. Knowing that those things which have been put on through the activities of the elements within thine own forces of thy body and mind are but as the stepping-stones to the knowledge that God is in and through *all* and in Him ye live and move and have thy being. When this is fully comprehended, fully understood, ye have the working knowledge of God in the earth.   281-34

As already noted, chapter fourteen begins with presence of the Lamb, being accompanied by the 144,000 that have the Father's name written in their foreheads. It is only by putting one's self in accord with the mind of the universal Christ Consciousness that individuals can proceed to the next level of attunement. The 144,000 that are called "virgins" in the Revelation text and being "without fault" are simply the perfected cells within the twelve structures of the body, waiting to quicken the whole.

The new song being sung by this group (Revelation 14:3) represents the new experience of being in accord with the spirit that is made available to each individual that reaches this level. They too become purified and cleansed and worthy to stand before the throne of God.

The fall of Babylon (Revelation 14:8) is associated with the fall of the supremacy of the lower self. Once this occurs, the mark of the beast can be overcome. However, the Revelation makes it clear that in spite of this level of personal attainment the individual is not finished. The activity of the angels with the sickles and the reaping (Revelation 14:15-19) corresponds to the new task set before those who have spiritualized themselves to this level—symbolized by the angels. According to the Cayce information, rather then resting they must now make themselves available in active service, sowing and reaping for the benefit of the rest of humankind (281-36). Further refinement, purification, and fermenting is required—all symbolized by the cultivation of grapes and the winepress (Revelation 18:20).

In spite of this level of purification and transformation, however, the work of the initiate is still not yet complete. At this point the individual is about to face the ultimate meeting of self dealing with the karmic patterns and memories of each of the seven centers, represented in the Revelation text by the seven final plagues.

REVELATION 15-16: SEVEN ANGELS WITH SEVEN VIALS—MEETING THE KARMIC MEMORY OF THE SEVEN CENTERS

This portion of the Revelation text can be referred to as the fifth sequence and essentially corresponds with the meeting of karmic patterns within the individual. As suggested by Revelation 15:8: "no man was able to enter into the temple, till the seven plagues of the seven angels was fulfilled," there can be no further movement toward an awareness of the divine until these memories have been dealt with. From Cayce's perspective, the soul memory receptacles that correspond to each of the seven centers are symbolized by the seven vials. As these memory patterns are poured out upon the earth (brought to the awareness of the individual) they must be healed, purified, or transformed. The Bible refers to this activity as the fulfilling of every jot and tittle (Matthew 5:18); the readings identify it as the "fulfilling of the law." (281-36) The conflict that occurs between the spiritual nature of the soul and the material urges that have been acquired in the earth is in fact the battle of Armageddon that occurs within each individual.

The "temple of the tabernacle of the testimony in heaven" being opened (Revelation 15:5) is associated with the Book of Life or the Akashic Records containing the record of the soul's past being revealed to the individual. In Cayce's cosmology, karma is essentially memory. Therefore, the soul memories related to each of the seven centers must be met. In 1940, while explaining how karmic memory could be met by each individual, Edgar Cayce told a fifty-two-year-old teacher that it was not necessary to live out this meeting of self in the earth. Instead, it could be accomplished at the level of spirit:

> Not that every soul shall not give account for the deeds done in the body, and in the body meet them! but in each meeting, in *each* activity, let the pattern—(not in self, not in mind alone, but in Him)—be the guide.
>
> As to the outlet, as to the manner of expression . . . there must be the quickening of the spirit.   2067-2

In the same reading, Cayce provided some encouraging advice regarding how the Christ Consciousness exemplified by Jesus actually provided a pattern of behavior for every soul: "He alone is each soul pattern. He *alone* is each soul pattern! *He* is thy *karma,* if ye put thy trust *wholly* in Him!" Essentially the implication is that an individual's karmic memory can be met at the level of spiritual awareness rather than living it out at the physical and mental levels.

The interpretation of each of the plagues is essentially the same in that they deal with the purification, conquering, and cleansing of "errors" and selfishness that have been a part of the soul's movement through time and space (281-36). The spiritual initiate being further healed of uncleanness within self is symbolized by the frogs coming out of the mouths of the dragon, the beast, and the false prophet (Revelation 16:13). Elsewhere, the Glad Helpers prayer group was told that the various horrors poured out upon the earth affecting the different elements were not to be taken as literal external events but as symbolical activities within the individual:

> . . . as the body elements that becomes conflicting one with another, which shows the overcoming within the individual activities of the influences that are constantly warring within . . . These are symbolical . . .   281-31

With the cleansing of the karmic patterns we come to the judgment of Babylon, symbolizing the lower self of the individual finally becoming known for what it is and consequently being overthrown.

REVELATION 17-20: THE FALL OF BABYLON— OVERTHROWING THE DOMINION OF THE LOWER SELF

Essentially, this section corresponds to the lower self being brought under control and becoming subservient to the higher self. In the sixth sequence both the city of Babylon and the woman of Babylon symbolize the lower self. Conversely, the seventh sequence portrays the purified higher self as both the bride and the New Jerusalem. The final purification process that occurs during this sixth sequence is what enables the dominion of the lower self to finally pass to a higher authority.

The whore of Babylon symbolizes how the soul in its passage through time and space has become overwhelmed ("drunken") by its own desires, power, and selfishness. The seven mountains or seven heads of the beast that she sits upon (Revelation 17:9) represents her seat of power and dominion over each of the seven centers of the body. The imagery indicates that the desires of the lower self have become the ruling force in the individual. These selfish desires must eventually become subservient to the higher self.

Keeping in mind that a horn can be symbolic of desire, the ten horns that represent ten kings of one mind that war with the woman and yet also give their power and strength to the beast may be indicative of the conflicting urges within each of the five senses that continually war with one another (Revelation 17:12). Paraphrasing Deuteronomy 30:15 and Matthew 26:41, members of the Glad Helpers prayer group were reminded how this played out within the individual:

> How has it been said? "O today there is life and death, good and evil—Choose thou." This may be said to be symbolical then of these conflicting forces within influences that are ever present, or as given by another, "The Spirit is willing, the flesh is weak."   281-31

In spite of the power of this conflict and the influence of the individual's desires, the Revelation text makes it clear that the authority of the lower self shall be overcome by the Lamb—the universal Christ Consciousness. However, rather then thinking that the lower self is somehow evil or bad, the readings suggest instead that it can been viewed as a experiential level that all individuals must encounter in their own process of spiritual growth and development. This experiential level is portrayed as the city of Babylon and described as: "those periods through which every soul passes in its delving into the varied mysteries that are the experiences of the carnal-mental, the spiritual-mental forces of the body . . . " (281-16) The challenge seems to be not whether the lower self exists but instead how long the individual allows it to reign supreme.

Finally being able to overcome the attraction and addiction to these selfish desires and the dominion of the lower self is the central message of the Revelation 18 text. Whether it's the imagery of the people being encouraged to leave the city (Revelation 18:4) or the fact that no one would purchase the city's merchandise any longer (Revelation 18:11), this sequence makes it clear that the city has lost its allure. This becomes clearly evident when Revelation 18:14 states, "And the fruits that thy soul lusted after are departed from thee . . . "

In part, the allure of the lower self is overcome because the soul learns that this lower level of existence is out of accord with its ultimate purposes and desires. Being involved at this level can only build habit patterns, desires, and shortcomings that eventually must be conquered because of the internal "hell" or suffering that they create within the individual. Edgar Cayce frequently stated that even Jesus learned obedience to the higher law through the things that He suffered. Although leaving behind these desires might appear to be challenging to the individual, we are told instead to "rejoice" for the dominion of the city has been cast down (Revelation 18:20-21). After the lower self has been put aside, once again the four beasts and the four and twenty elders bow down, becoming subservient so that the Revelation attunement can continue (Revelation 19:4).

We next discover that the time for the marriage of the bride to the Lamb has arrived. According to the readings, the bride being adorned in clean, white linen (Revelation 19:8) portrays the fact that the individual has become so raised in spiritual consciousness "as to become as a new being." (281-36) The purity of the soul has been reestablished. Now the marriage—the integration with the divine—can take place within the individual.

At this level of attainment, the white horse upon which sits one called "Faithful and True" is now the messenger of attunement and the spirit of the universal Christ Consciousness or ideal that pervades the entire body. Elsewhere, the readings identified this universal Christ ideal as: " . . . the awareness within each soul, imprinted in pattern on the mind and waiting to be awakened by the will, of the soul's oneness with God." (5749-14)

As an interesting aside, Cayce identified the "fellow servant" that also knew the testimony of Jesus (Revelation 19:10) as the soul of

Peter, who came to John during his Revelation experience. The readings explained that this communication exemplified, in part, the fact that all individuals who undertake this process of purification and spiritualization avail of themselves the Revelation experience (281-37). Previously, the prayer group had been told that before his death Peter had made a promise to John that this portion of the Revelation fulfilled, "I will endeavor to keep thee in remembrance; even after my death I will return to you." (281-16)

The imagery of fire in the Revelation text represents both a purification and a purging process. Therefore, the imagery of the beast and the false prophet being cast into the lake of fire (Revelation 19:20) suggests that both the rebellious spirit and the immature self must remain in a state of perpetual purification. Because of the power of free will, these two aspects of the self evidently remain as potentials within each individual and are only kept under control by ongoing vigilance and by remaining true to the higher self and one's attunement to the divine.

Although the readings frequently stressed the fact that the foremost interpretation of John's Revelation was one that correlates the imagery with the physical body, on several occasions Cayce stated that there were additional ways to interpret biblical symbolism. For example, in March 1937 Cayce told members of the Glad Helpers prayer group:

> In giving the interpretation of this particular portion of the Revelation, it must all be kept in mind that, as has been indicated, while many of the references—or all—refer to the physical body as the pattern, there is that as may be said to be the literal and the spiritual and the metaphysical interpretation of almost all portions of the Scripture, and especially of the Revelation as given by John.
>
> Yet all of these to be true, to be practical, to be applicable in the experiences of individuals . . .   281-31

Having more than one possible interpretation for some of the symbolism is clearly suggested, for example, in Revelation 20. The imagery of the dragon being bound in the bottomless pit for a thousand years is suggestive of the rebellious spirit being contained for a time within the confines of the lower self. On the other hand, the readings state this imagery also indicates that anyone still possessing the rebellious spirit will literally be forbidden to incarnate in the earth for a thousand years. What this means is that there will come a time in the history of the world when only those souls who have chosen a higher spiritual ideal will be allowed to reincarnate, enabling them to make much greater progress in their own spiritual development. Afterward, the ban will be lifted and those souls who are still wrestling with their lower nature will be allowed to return and continue their own spiritual development. Comparing the importance of those spiritually minded souls who will be allowed to return with the importance of the 144,000 perfected cells within the body, Cayce urged individuals to, "Be *ye ALL determined* within thy minds, thy hearts, thy purposes, to be of that number." (281-37)

Examining some of the remaining symbolism in chapter twenty portrays how the book of life (or the Akashic Records/soul memory) of the individual evaluates and measures everything about the soul so that eventually only that which is in keeping with the higher self is worthy to stand before God. Although this might appear frightening to the personality level of an individual, it is simply part of the process of gaining an awareness of the ultimate self and self's relationship to the divine.

The "second death" (Revelation 20:14) referred to in the text is essentially once again becoming subservient to the desires and fears of the lower self in spite of having obtained for a time a higher level of understanding and awareness. Having death cast into the lake of fire suggests that even this tendency will be kept in abeyance by ongoing vigilance and attunement to the divine.

REVELATION 21-22: A NEW HEAVEN AND A NEW EARTH—ASCENDANCY OF THE HIGHER SELF

The seventh and final sequence portrays the fact that the personal revelation process has been completed, the higher self has become the dominant influence and the individual has become transformed: "And I saw a new heaven and a new earth; for the first heaven and the first earth were passed away." (Revelation 21:1)

In the imagery, John is carried away "in the spirit to a great and high mountain" (Revelation 21:10), suggesting that during his meditation experience he rose in consciousness to an even higher level of attunement. From this place he is able to perceive the purity and wonder of the new Jerusalem.

Edgar Cayce stated that the city of Jerusalem had long been regarded as "the holy place, the holy city" and therefore was an appropriate symbol for the higher self and the soul's higher purposes and experiences (281-37). Building upon earlier symbolism, the twelve gates of the city (or the twelve foundations) can correspond to the twelve purified structures of the body or the purified pathways of the twelve pairs of cranial nerves. In addition, the number twelve correlates to the twelve tribes (or the twelve Apostles) and at this point is suggestive of a perfected response pattern in every structure of the body as well as in every area of the individual's life. At this level of attainment the individual's responses are no longer for the seeking of self. Instead, the individual has become an integral part of the activities of the divine.

The golden reed that John is given with which to measure the city (Revelation 21:15) is symbolic of the divine understanding and purpose he now possesses. The precious stones that adorn the city's foundation walls (Revelation 21:19-20) are symbolic of the perfection and great worth that have been achieved through hardship. In the same manner, the twelve pearls on the twelve gates (Revelation 21:21) correspond to wisdom and enlightenment. The fact that the night shall be no more (Revelation 21:25) suggests that for an individual at this level of attainment there can be no more separation from the light of the divine. As indicated by the text and Revelation 21:27, at this level of awareness the individual will no longer be susceptible to the dominion of the lower self.

The final chapter of Revelation portrays the fact that there will come a time within the individual (as well as within the world as a whole) when everything that exists will be in continuous attunement with this universal Christ ideal—the Lamb. Cayce stated that the symbolism of the "pure river of water of life, clear as crystal" (Revelation 22:1), was actually symbolic of "the active flow of the purpose of the souls of men made pure in same." (281-37) As indicated by Revelation 22:2, there will no longer be a season when the activities of individuals (and the earth) can bring forth anything but the best fruit. There will no longer be a time when individually any portion of the self is at war or collectively when the nations of the earth are in conflict. The light of God will have become so manifest that all other lights will seem pale by comparison.

Once John reaches this level of attainment he is told that the process of personal revelation is left up to the individual and cannot be forced upon another: "He that is unjust, let him be unjust still: and he which is filthy, let him be filthy still: and he that is righteous, let him be righteous still: and he that is holy, let him be holy still." (Revelation 22:11) However, rather than being made available only to a select few, both the Revelation text and the words of Jesus confirm the existence of this transformational process for every soul—a metamorphosis that is part of the soul's ultimate connection to God. In the words of Jesus:

> They are not of the world, even as I am not of the world . . .
> That they all may be one; as thou, Father, art in me, and I in thee, that they also may be one in us: that the world may believe that thou hast sent me.
>   And the glory which thou gavest me I have given them; that they may be one, even as we are one . . .
>   (John 17:16, 21-22)

And the Revelation text states: "He that overcometh shall inherit all things; and I will be his God, and he shall be my son." (Revelation 21:7)

In a similar manner the Edgar Cayce readings suggest that spiritual transformation is simply the attainment of the soul's birthright. From Cayce's perspective, the nature of humankind is one in which each individual is a *spiritual being* presently taking part in a *physical experience*. Therefore, as the lower self is put aside in preference for the higher self, the divinity of the soul becomes manifest. Obviously, this "revelation of self" exists as a potential within every individual.

In spite of the symbolism of Revelation appearing challenging to understand, Cayce believed that any sincere study of the text would result in the individual becoming more meek, more patient, more humble, and more in accord with the fruits of the spirit. Ultimately, that was the purpose of John's revelation. It was not to create confusion or even mystery. It was not to provide a prophetic calendar of cataclysmic events destined to befall some future generation of humankind. Instead, it was to present all individuals with a revelation of what they ultimately sought while providing the sequential process they needed to follow in order to find it within themselves.

As was first discovered by a small prayer group in Virginia Beach, Virginia, the Edgar Cayce approach to the Book of Revelation becomes relevant to all of humankind. Through a symbolic exploration of archetypal images, patterns, and processes, John's visionary experience portrays the means through which each individual can awaken to a higher state of consciousness and the pattern of wholeness that exists as potential within the self. In other words, the Revelation is the ultimate manual for self-discovery. Through a series of steps that include setting aside the lower self, personal evaluation and purification, establishing a spiritual ideal, and facing everything within the individual that is out of accord with the workings of the spirit, the nature of the soul can become manifest in the earth. Essentially, the Revelation of John is the revelation of how each and every individual can attain to an awareness of the universal Christ Consciousness while in the earth.

8

Archetypal Imagery and Revelation Symbolism

The Book of Revelation utilizes symbolism to illustrate the connections between John's visionary experience and the process of spiritual awakening occurring within his body and consciousness. The various conflicts that occur within the Revelation text symbolically portray the warring impulses existing within each individual as the motivations for self-gratification, self-preservation, self-propagation, and self-sustenance are directed instead toward greater spiritual awareness and attunement. This overall process of spiritual awakening occurs as the lower self is made subservient to the higher self. It follows a pattern of progressive development that has relevance for all individuals, regardless of their creed, race, or period of existence in history. From this perspective, the Revelation symbolism is therefore universal or archetypal in nature.

Since John's vision on Patmos encapsulates an archetypal experience that is accessible to all of humankind, it should be anticipated that similar patterns and symbols from the Revelation might be found elsewhere. In other words, John's experiences with the rebellious spirit (symbolized, in part, by the dragon), with the seven spiritual centers of the body (symbolized, in part, by the seven-sealed book), and with the four lower motivations (symbolized, in part, by the four beasts) would have comparable examples in human history. The process of passing through various stages of purification and attunement would have similar correlations, as well. In fact, a variety of examples utilizing comparable archetypal imagery to that found in Revelation can be discovered in history, in myth, and even in fairy tale. Far from intending to encompass every occurrence, what follows are just a few instances illustrating this phenomenon.

For thousands of years the ancient Egyptians utilized ornate rituals and ceremonies designed to insure the safe passage of the Pharaoh from the mundane world of humankind to the afterlife world of the gods. In time one of those ceremonies became the process of mummification, which the Egyptians believed was crucial in making the transition to the afterlife. During this process, Egyptian embalmers removed some of the body's internal organs, dried them, and placed them safely in four vases, referred to as canopic jars. It was believed that the body's organs would be necessary in the next world and this process would enable the organs to eventually be restored to the body. Each of these canopic jars possessed a head-shaped lid covering the organs. Generally, the heads were fashioned to represent the four sons of the god Horus: a falcon, a jackal, a man, and a baboon. Each of these four creatures can be associated with the four beasts of the Revelation.

Just as the four lower beasts of the Revelation become instrumental in enabling the initiate to attune to higher consciousness, the four sons of Horus become instrumental in enabling the deceased Pharaoh to make the transition from death to the afterlife. The correlation between these two sets of four and the four lower spiritual centers or endocrine glands can be easily identified. For example, both the falcon son of Horus and the eagle of Revelation, as winged-creatures elevated above the earth, correspond to the highest portion of the lower self or the center associated with the thymus. The aggressive nature of the jackal is similar to the predatory instincts of the lion and both correspond to the adrenals. The man-shaped canopic jar is identical to the man in the Revelation text and both correspond to the cells of Leydig. Finally, both the baboon son of Horus and the calf from Revelation represent the gonad center, which is associated with sexuality. The rationale is that throughout history the cow has often been connected with the goddess of fertility (e.g., the Egyptian goddess Hathor, the Celtic goddess Damona, the Greek goddess Hera, the Phoenician goddess Astarte, etc.), whereas the playfulness of the baboon might correspond to the playfulness of the human creature when it comes to the activity of sexuality (e.g., only the human creature engages in sexual activity for more than procreation).

This use of four creatures or beasts is certainly not limited to Revelation and the Egyptians. In fact, Swiss psychologist Carl Jung pointed out that animals and groups of four are universal symbols, frequently appearing in both religious and cultural symbolism. (Jung, *Man and His Symbols,* pg. 5) For example, Chinese tradition claims the existence of four supernatural creatures: the dragon, the Phoenix, the unicorn, and the tortoise. These creatures are often utilized in Chinese art and each of these mythological creatures is said to represent all other animals.

In trying to compare these Chinese creatures with those in Revelation we might be tempted to correlate the Phoenix with the eagle, since both are creatures of flight; however, the Chinese associate each of these mythic animals with various traits and inclinations, and those descriptions provide a much closer parallel. According to Chinese tradition, the Phoenix can be associated with the union of yin and yang, the balance of male-female energies and sexuality. For that reason, the Phoenix more closely corresponds with the center associated with the cells of Leydig. The tortoise can be a symbol for longevity, persistence, and immorality and is therefore an appropriate symbol for the gonads. According to legend, the Chinese unicorn could distinguish between the guilty and the innocence; consequently it could represent the level of the adrenals. Interestingly enough, the unicorn is also sometimes replaced by the Chinese symbol of the white tiger, providing an appropriate symbol for this level. Finally, the dragon is known to live part of its time in the earth and part in the heavens. In fact, to the Chinese the dragon can symbolize the regenerative power of heaven. Therefore, the dragon could be associated with the level of the thymus.

In addition to creatures and beasts being used to symbolize aspects of the self in the process of transformation, similar thematic components dealing with the spiritualization of the lower self can be shown to exist in art, architecture, and legend. Perhaps one of the most famous examples in art is depicted in Michelangelo's ceiling of the Sistine Chapel in the Vatican. One of the frequently duplicated paintings from this masterpiece portrays God's outstretched finger reaching out to touch the hand of Adam, suggesting that the divine may ever be within reach of humankind. Another example that illustrates the gradual process of purification and attunement depicted in John's vision dealing with the ascendancy of the higher self and personal communication with the divine can be seen in the physical layout of the rabbinical Temple at Jerusalem.

Historically, the Temple was essentially laid out in three structures: the outer court, the inner court, and the holy of holies. The outer court of the temple was used as a gathering place for all of the Jewish people. The Temple services of the priests were conducted in the inner court. The holiest place of the Temple was the holy of holies, where God could be found. One's level of spiritual purity (and corresponding stature in the priesthood) is what enabled an individual to move ever closer to the place where God was said to dwell. The Temple itself was designed as a place where it was possible to meet god face-to-face. Only the High Priest, however, was allowed to enter into the holy of holies and then only once a year, on the Day of Atonement, after having undergone a complex ritual of prayer and purification (Jewish Encyclopedia, vol. XI, pgs. 92-95).

These three main components of the temple (outer court or courtyard, inner court or holy place, and the holy of holies or dwelling place of the Ark of the Covenant) correspond to the three levels of consciousness depicted in the Edgar Cayce information. The Cayce readings describe these levels as the conscious mind, the subconscious mind, and the superconscious mind. It is at this highest level of the mind that an individual in deep prayer or meditation (such as John on the Isle of Patmos) can meet God face to face. These correlations between the body, the temple, and the possibility of meeting God within have numerous examples in both the Cayce readings and the Bible, including:

From the Edgar Cayce material:

> For indeed thy body is the temple of the living God. It is the temple of thine own awareness.   826-11

> But thy body is the temple of the living God, and He has promised to meet thee in thine own tabernacle; for the kingdom is within and there He hath promised to meet thee!   1632-2

And, from the Bible:

> And when he was demanded of the Pharisees, when the kingdom of God should come, he answered them and said, "The kingdom of God cometh not with observation: Neither shall they say, Lo here! or, lo there! for, behold, the kingdom of God is within you."   (Luke 17:20-21)

> For this commandment which I command thee this day, it is not hidden from thee, neither is it far off.
> It is not in heaven, that thou shouldest say, Who shall go up for us to heaven, and bring it unto us, that we may hear it, and do it?
> Neither is it beyond the sea, that thou shouldest say, Who shall go over the sea for us, and bring it unto us, that we may hear it, and do it?
> But the word is very nigh unto thee, in thy mouth, and in thy heart, that thou mayest do it.
>   (Deuteronomy 30:11-14)

In John's Revelation, it is only after the rebelliousness of the lower self has been overcome that John's consciousness perceives that the bride (the New Jerusalem) is now worthy to marry the Lamb—the Christ (Revelation 21). The symbolism suggested by this imagery is that John's consciousness has finally become so purified that he is now worthy to become identified with the universal Christ Consciousness. This process of overcoming the lower self and then becoming worthy to "marry" the Christ is also chronicled in the popular mythic tale of Saint George and the Dragon, as well as its Greek counterpart Perseus and Andromeda.

The story of St. George and the Dragon begins with an evil dragon threatening a small kingdom. According to the story, the only thing that the people of the kingdom can do each day to appease the dragon's wrath is to feed sheep to the dragon. Unfortunately, one day the kingdom runs out of sheep and the people decide they have no choice but to sacrifice one of their own people. In order to decide who will become the dragon's victim, the people throw lots and the fated lot falls to the King's only daughter, a virgin. The king objects and tries to buy a substitute to stand in his daughter's place but the people refuse. To appease the dragon, the virgin daughter is dressed as a bride and led to the place where the dragon receives its sacrifice.

Luckily, St. George arrives just moments before the dragon. Rather than following the princess's request for him to leave instead of perishing along with her, St. George remains. When the dragon arrives, St. George makes the sign of the cross and fights and subdues the dragon. Borrowing the princess's girdle, St. George puts the girdle around the dragon's neck and the princess leads the dragon back into the kingdom. Because of the St. George's victory, all of the people are persuaded to convert to Christianity. After their baptism, the dragon is beheaded. In exchange for his courage and gallantry, St. George is offered half of the king's kingdom but George refuses and bids the king farewell as he continues on his journey.

Apart from any literal elements of the tale, for St. George (the patron Saint of Great Britain and elsewhere) was said to have actually lived in the fourth century, the archetypal symbolism of the story is very similar to John's Revelation. Essentially, the dragon can be identified with the seven-headed beast or the lower self of the Revelation text. The princess is associated with the bride of the Lamb. Obviously,

St. George represents a champion of the Christ. He can also be associated with the archangel Michael in the Revelation who overthrows the beast. In the Saint George story it is only after the people of the kingdom ascribe to spirituality and a higher ideal (e.g., becoming baptized) that the dragon and the rebelliousness of the lower self are destroyed. The Greek version of Perseus and Andromeda is very similar except for some minor details such as the fact that the story predates Christianity, the monster in the Greek legend is a sea-dragon, and the characters of Perseus and Andromeda marry in the end.

In addition to history and legend, universal symbolism is often depicted in classical fairy tales, enabling the archetypal patterns of the self to be never truly forgotten. For example, Edgar Cayce's son, Hugh Lynn, frequently pointed out how the fairy tale story of *Snow White and the Seven Dwarfs* had numerous parallels with the symbolism of John's Revelation. First attributed to the Brothers' Grimm in the nineteenth century, the story of Snow White was later immortalized by Walt Disney in his 1937 cartoon classic. Hugh Lynn believed that Snow White was an archetypal symbol of spirit coming into matter and getting into a body containing seven spiritual centers, represented by the seven dwarfs. The overall story and some of its archetypal significance can be described as follows:

In the tale, Snow White is the daughter of a royal king and queen and therefore a princess in her own rite. Unfortunately the queen dies and the king remarries, causing Snow White to acquire a stepmother queen. This stepmother possesses a magic mirror that repeatedly tells her that she is the fairest in all the land. The mirror holds fast to its assessment of the stepmother's beauty until Snow White reaches a certain age. In the Grimm version of the story that age is interestingly enough seven years old. After Snow White has come of age and the stepmother asks her recurring question, the mirror's response suddenly changes to say that although the stepmother is fair, "Snow White is a thousand times more fair." (Manheim, pg. 184) The response puts the stepmother into a rage and she orders a huntsman to take the girl into the forest and kill her, bringing back her lungs and liver (the Disney version substitutes her heart) as proof that the girl is dead. The huntsman has pity on the girl and sets her free. He kills a wild animal in order to satisfy the organ requirement set down by the stepmother.

In the Disney version, Snow White arrives at a small cottage and wipes clean a window in order to peer inside. The whole place is a mess. There are soiled clothes all over the place. Cobwebs and dust fill the room and there are dirty dishes in the sink. Hugh Lynn Cayce used to suggest that this beautifully depicted the average state of the subconscious mind. The girl cleans the whole place up with the help of some of the animals from the forest. The house also possesses seven tiny chairs and seven tiny beds, causing Snow White to believe that children inhabit the cottage. After cleaning the house and preparing dinner, Snow White falls asleep. While she is still sleeping, the seven dwarfs return from their day of work. In the Disney version, the dwarfs are Doc, Sleepy, Happy, Sneezy, Grumpy, Bashful, and Dopey.

Building upon the same correlation proposed by Hugh Lynn Cayce, Dr. Gladys McGarey connects the seven dwarfs with each of the seven spiritual centers, as follows:

- Dopey is associated with the gonad center. Among all of the dwarfs, he was the fastest dancer and had more energy than all the rest. When the dwarfs were all being kissed by Snow White, he was the only one to line up three times.
- Bashful is connected to the cells of Leydig. The rationale is that one of the first things that often makes us shy and bashful is our sexual differentiation.
- Grumpy is a perfect symbol for the adrenals. One of the things that make us most irritable is when others try to interfere with our personal power.
- Sneezy symbolizes the thymus. This is the air center—whatever Sneezy breathed in had to be sneezed out.
- Happy is connected to the joyful use of the will and the will is associated with the thyroid center.
- Sleepy corresponds to the pineal, the center which is associated with day-night cycles and light.
- Finally, Doc is the head dwarf and therefore represents the master gland, the pituitary.

(McGarey, pgs. 19-24)

In the story, the bliss of Snow White and her seven little friends is short-lived. Once again the stepmother returns to her magic mirror and rather than hearing that she has regained her title as the fairest one of all, the evil woman learns that Snow White is still very much alive. In the Grimms' version of the story, the stepmother makes three different attempts on Snow White's life. These attempts, described below, can be correlated with the three woes of the Revelation as well as the three temptations of Jesus (Matthew 4). They are essentially the tests of the physical, the mental, and the spiritual aspects of the self.

In the physical test, the stepmother disguises herself as an old peddler woman and convinces Snow White to purchase a blouse that is tied with lace. Snow White agrees and puts on the blouse, which the stepmother ties too tight. The tight laces cut off Snow White's breathing and she passes out and is left for dead. The stepmother leaves and eventually the dwarfs come home. It does not take the dwarfs long to realize what has happened. As a result, they cut the lace, enabling Snow White to breathe and return to consciousness.

When the stepmother discovers that Snow is still alive, the time arrives for another test. In this second attempt on the girl's life the stepmother disguises herself as an old woman and approaches the cottage with a pretty poison hair comb for sale. In symbolism, the hair is often associated with thoughts and ideas, therefore this corresponds to the mental test. Unaware of the danger, Snow White allows the old woman to place the poison comb in her hair, resulting in the girl falling into a dead faint. The stepmother departs, convinced that Snow White is finally dead. However, when the dwarfs return they remove the comb and Snow White awakens.

The stepmother is livid when she discovers from the mirror that Snow White is still alive. In the Grimms' versions, she screams that Snow White must die, "Even if it costs me my own life." (Manheim, pg. 188) This time the stepmother disguises herself as a peasant woman and brings a poison apple to the cottage for sale. Symbolically, the apple is reminiscent of the spiritual fall of Adam and Eve; therefore this is the spiritual test that Snow White faces. Unwilling to be tricked a third time, Snow White refuses to eat the apple. However, the stepmother has cleverly poisoned only half of the apple—the reddest half.

When the old woman cuts the apple in half and takes a bite out of her half, Snow White is tricked into taking a bite out of the other half. The result is that the girl falls dead to the floor. The stepmother departs and is pleased to learn that her mirror has finally renamed her "the fairest in the land." This time when the dwarfs return they are powerless to revive the maiden.

Unable to bring themselves to bury her in the earth, the dwarfs fashion a glass coffin so that others will always be able to gaze upon the girl's beauty. In the Grimms' version, Snow White lays in her coffin as one dead for many, many years. One day a prince comes by and sees Snow White in her coffin. So taken by the young woman's beauty, the prince finally convinces the dwarfs to let him have the coffin. As fate would have it, as they begin to move the coffin, they stumble and Snow White is shaken, causing the piece of the poison apple to come out of her mouth. Snow White awakens and is married to the prince. (In the Disney version, Snow White is awakened after simply being kissed by the prince.) After awakening, the prince and Snow White are destined to marry and live happily ever after. (As an aside, in the Grimms' version the evil stepmother is forced to fulfill her sworn oath by being made to dance at the couple's wedding wearing red-hot iron slippers until she falls dead to the floor.)

In addition to what has already been stated, Snow White can represent the spirit's descent into matter and being overwhelmed by the tests of the physical, the mental, and the spiritual. Because of her essential failure of each of these tests, she becomes forever trapped in a perpetual state of unconsciousness in the earth. This essentially corresponds with the soul becoming unconscious of its spiritual essence while incarnate in the earth. It is only with the presence of the universal Christ Consciousness, symbolized by the prince, that the soul is revived and allowed to return to its rightful state of nobility in a royal kingdom. Interestingly enough, in the Disney version each of the dwarfs is raised up by the prince (the universal Christ) and kissed good-bye by Snow White who sits upon a majestic horse. Symbolically, this seems to suggest that only after each of the centers has been purified and raised up by the universal Christ Consciousness can the soul return to an awareness of its divine origins.

Snow White's journey is similar to that of the Prodigal Son (Luke 15:11-24) in which the soul travels on a journey of experiences and challenges that eventually lead to regaining its rightful inheritance and its proper place called Home. Additional stories that can be shown to illustrate this archetypal pattern of the soul's journey include such works as *The Hobbit, Pilgrim's Progress, The Adventures of Pinocchio, The Wizard of Oz,* and others. In the case of *The Wizard of Oz,* for example, much of the universal symbolism found in John's Revelation is portrayed. In this well-known story the four lower centers can be associated with the four travelers on the road to Oz: the tin man, the lion, Dorothy, and the scarecrow depicting the thymus, the adrenals, the cells of Leydig, and the gonads, respectively. In addition, Glinda, the good witch, can portray the higher self and the wizard in Oz can correspond to the false prophet stage of spiritual development, just to name a few. This illustrates how classical stories can often depict archetypal patterns of human experience that frequently remain just beyond the bounds of conscious awareness, yet become memorable because they clearly portray something universal about the human condition.

To be sure, the fact that patterns and symbols of universal experience can be found in stories, in legend, and in myth throughout history doesn't necessarily suggest that authors, architects, and artists are consciously aware of the archetypal significance of their works. In other words, the Brothers' Grimm and Walt Disney would probably be very surprised to hear about the similarities between the symbolism of Revelation and *Snow White*, for example. The same holds true for the divinely inspired layout of the Jewish Temple or the way in which the story of St. George and the Dragon was handed down by mythic storytellers for generations. Instead, these correlations generally occur not due to intention but rather because the symbols of archetypes and universal patterns of human experience exist deep within the subconscious realms of the mind—the very realm from which the imagination, storytelling, legend, and even divine inspiration are often given birth.

9

Meditation, the Physical Body, and the Lord's Prayer

John's symbolic experience of the Book of Revelation portrays the process of spiritual awakening and attunement as it was occurring within his body and consciousness. Essentially the imagery depicts the internal conflicts and struggles that transpire between the spiritual awareness of an individual's ultimate connection and oneness with the divine and his or her lower self consciousness that may feel threatened for survival. It is a transformational process that every soul will eventually encounter since it is a process that enables the individual to awaken to her or his higher and true self.

Because the seven endocrine glands (gonads, cells of Leydig, adrenals, thymus, thyroid, pineal, and pituitary) serve as conduits of energy between the spiritual chakras and the physical body, individuals may consider how they might work with the centers in order to stimulate their own soul development and spiritual awakening. Some-

times individuals might even wonder about the advisability of medi-
tating upon the spiritual centers or attempting such things as deep
breathing exercises to specifically open the centers, and so forth. Actually, the Cayce readings advised against such practices because they
can sometimes inadvertently open the individual up to experiences
and memories that could be harmful rather than helpful. However,
from the perspective of the Edgar Cayce material, there is an optimum
process for awakening spiritual awareness at the level of each of the
centers. That process was demonstrated by John's visionary experience, resulting in the symbolism of the Revelation. Perhaps surprisingly, Cayce suggested that this same optimal progression had also
been pointed out by Jesus to his Apostles in the form of the Lord's
Prayer. Apparently it is a form of prayer that not only stimulates
attunement but somehow also addresses each of the spiritual centers
in a constructive manner.

According to scripture when Jesus was in Galilee with his Apostles,
He took them aside and shortly after discussing the Beatitudes (e.g.,
"blessed are the peacemakers . . . ") he suggested that there was a way
that they could personally pray to God. He advised that they enter into
a place of quiet and use the following prayer:

> Our Father which art in heaven, Hallowed be thy name.
> Thy kingdom come. Thy will be done in earth, as it is in
> heaven. Give us this day our daily bread. And forgive us
> our debts, as we forgive our debtors. And lead us not into
> temptation, but deliver us from evil: For thine is the king-
> dom, and the power, and the glory, forever. Amen.
>   (Matthew 6:9-13; alternately Luke 11:2-4)

As will be described, this prayer apparently promotes the optimum
movement of the kundalini energy during meditation. It provides a
balanced approach to addressing the seven spiritual centers, enabling
the energy to pass through each center in a manner that does not
awaken negative behavioral patterns or karmic memories that might
be harmful to the individual. This approach essentially uses the Lord's
Prayer as a tool for focusing awareness at the level of each of the
spiritual centers. Cayce suggested that when this prayer was used ap-

propriately it enabled individuals from every background and religious denomination to better understand their relationship to the Creative Forces, essentially because of the archetypal nature of the prayer and the symbolism and awareness that could be quickened within self.

When members of the Glad Helpers prayer group asked Cayce whether or not the version of the prayer provided by scriptures was an accurate translation, Cayce replied in part: "Make its purpose and its intent a portion of thine self. For, there be many misinterpretations, poor translations, but to find fault with that thou hast and not use same is to make excuses that you haven't it as it was given." (281-20) In other words, they were encouraged to simply use the prayer as it existed and to see for themselves what kind of results they experienced. The suggestion was to use the prayer essentially as a method of attunement by *feeling* the meaning of each phrase within the corresponding spiritual center. In the language of the Cayce readings:

> As in feeling, as it were, the flow of the meanings of each portion of same throughout the body-physical. For as there is the response to the mental representations of all of these in the *mental* body, it may build into the physical body in the manner as He, thy Lord, thy Brother, so well expressed in, "I have bread ye know not of."   281-29

This suggestion of *feeling* a specific awareness throughout the spiritual centers was also given to a thirty-three-year-old music teacher who wanted to know how he could increase the activity within each of his chakras as a means of attaining to "higher mental and spiritual powers." Cayce advised him that rather than trying to force his spiritual centers open, he should instead meditate upon the thought, *"Not my will but thine, O Lord, be done in and through me"* and to feel that awareness throughout each of the centers (1861-4).

Apparently this process of feeling a specific awareness within each of the spiritual centers somehow awakens an even deeper level of attunement and ultimately a greater awareness of the individual's relationship to the Creator. As a higher level of awareness is held at each center, overall spiritual attunement is somehow enhanced. With that in mind, the following diagram depicts each of the centers, the portion of the Lord's Prayer that Cayce stated addressed that center, and the corresponding awareness that might be most helpful to *feel* at that level during meditation and the recitation of the Lord's Prayer:

Using the Lord's Prayer in this manner addresses the higher three

The Lord's Prayer and the Seven Spiritual Centers

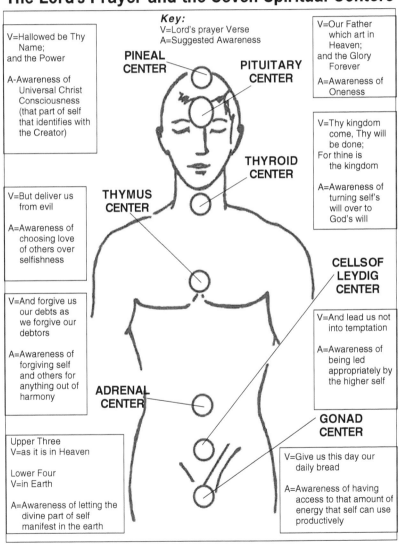

Key:
V=Lord's prayer Verse
A=Suggested Awareness

V=Hallowed be Thy Name;
and the Power

A-Awareness of Universal Christ Consciousness (that part of self that identifies with the Creator)

PINEAL CENTER

PITUITARY CENTER

V=Our Father which art in Heaven;
and the Glory Forever

A=Awareness of Oneness

V=Thy kingdom come, Thy will be done;
For thine is the kingdom

A=Awareness of turning self's will over to God's will

THYROID CENTER

V=But deliver us from evil

A=Awareness of choosing love of others over selfishness

THYMUS CENTER

CELLSOF LEYDIG CENTER

V=And forgive us our debts as we forgive our debtors

A=Awareness of forgiving self and others for anything out of harmony

V=And lead us not into temptation

A=Awareness of being led appropriately by the higher self

ADRENAL CENTER

GONAD CENTER

Upper Three
V=as it is in Heaven

Lower Four
V=in Earth

A=Awareness of letting the divine part of self manifest in the earth

V=Give us this day our daily bread

A=Awareness of having access to that amount of energy that self can use productively centers first, then the lower four, followed once again by the higher three. It is interesting to note that the sequence in which the four lower centers are addressed follows the same pattern in both the opening vision of the Revelation and in the Lord's Prayer: first the gonads, then the adrenals, then the cells of Leydig, and then the Thymus. To illustrate this further, the following chart shows the center, the respective verse from the Lord's Prayer, and finally the opening vision from Revelation:

Spiritual Center	Lord's Prayer Verse	Opening Vision
Gonads	Give us this day our daily bread	White Horse
Adrenals	And forgive us our debts as we forgive our debtors	Red Horse
Cells of Leydig	And lead us not into temptation	Black Horse
Thymus	But deliver us from evil temptation	Pale Horse

Ideally meditation is not a tool for clearing the mind, instead it is a process in which consciousness is focused in such a manner that a higher spiritual awareness or a spiritual ideal can be awakened throughout the body. Potentially, the Lord's Prayer can further heighten personal attunement by focusing spiritual awareness at the level of each of the spiritual centers. The following exercise has been provided for individuals interested in working with this information in a manner suggested by the Edgar Cayce readings.

MEDITATING WITH THE LORD'S PRAYER

If you would like to use the Lord's Prayer as a meditation tool as has been described above, the following steps provide one suggested approach.

1) Get comfortable in your chair (or sitting up on the floor) and close your eyes. Take a deep breath and begin to relax.
2) Edgar Cayce often suggested head-and-neck exercises to help with relaxation and attunement. Those exercises can be described as follows:

With your spine straight, drop your head forward gently toward the chest and then slowly bring it back upright in place. Do this slowly, three times.

Next, drop your head rearward gently and then bring it back upright in place. Do this slowly, three times.

Then, drop your head to the right, gently allowing your right ear to move in the direction of your shoulder. Bring it back in place. Do this slowly, three times.

Next, drop your head to the left, gently allowing your left ear to move in the direction of your shoulder. Bring it back in place. Do this slowly, three times.

Then, drop your head forward toward the chest and slowly rotate your head in a clockwise motion, passing by your right shoulder, your back, your left shoulder and finally back near your chest. Do this slowly, three times and then bring your head back in place.

Finally, drop your head forward toward the chest and then slowly rotate your head in a counterclockwise motion, passing by your left shoulder, your back, your right shoulder and finally back near your chest. Do this slowly, three times and then bring your head back in place.

3) Edgar Cayce also suggested that alternate breathing exercises could help with relaxation and attunement. He described those exercises as follows (you may wish to repeat the exercise three times):

> In breathing, take into the right nostril, strength! Exhale through thy mouth. Intake in thy left nostril, exhaling through the right; opening the centers of thy body . . .
>
> 281-28

4) Surround yourself with a spiritual thought or a prayer of protection. Possible thoughts might include, "Not my will but Thy will be done," and a prayer of protection might entail visualizing yourself surrounded by a white light or the presence of the universal Christ Consciousness.

5) Slowly say the Lord's Prayer. As you say the prayer, *feel* the meaning of the awareness listed for each of the centers, as follows:

Lord's Prayer Verse	Spiritual Center	Overall Awareness
Our Father which art in Heaven	Pituitary	Awareness of Oneness
Hallowed be Thy Name	Pineal	Awareness of universal Christ Consciousness (that part of self that identifies with the Creator)
Thy kingdom come, thy will be done	Thyroid	Awareness of turning self's will over to God's will
In Earth as it is in Heaven	Lower four; Upper three	Awareness of letting the divine part of self manifest in the earth
Give us this day our daily bread	Gonads	Awareness of having access to that amount of energy that self can use productively
And forgive us our debts as we forgive our debtors	Adrenals	Awareness of forgiving self and others for anything out of harmony
And lead us not into temptation	Cells of Leydig	Awareness of being led appropriately by the higher self
But deliver us from evil	Thymus	Awareness of choosing love of others over selfishness
For thine is the kingdom	Thyroid	Awareness of turning self's will over to God's will
And the Power	Pineal	Awareness of Universal Christ Consciousness (that part of self that identifies with the Creator)
And the Glory forever. Amen.	Pituitary	Awareness of Oneness

6) You may wish to focus on the *feeling* of this overall sense of oneness or perhaps an awareness of "Not my will but Thy will be done" as a means of extending your meditation period to between ten and fifteen minutes. If your mind wanders, simply bring it back to the appropriate feeling or awareness.

7) The Cayce readings recommend sending out prayers or positive thoughts to other people as a means of ending a meditation session and also becoming a channel of blessings to others.

8) Finally, in order to finish your meditation period, you may wish to take a deep breath, feeling firmly grounded in the present.

The Lord's Prayer is ideally suited for attunement and meditation because it specifically addresses each of the seven spiritual centers and moves the energy of meditation in the method most conducive to the overall health and wellbeing of the individual seeking attunement. Rather than trying to visualize any of the centers opening, Cayce recommended instead allowing the feeling and energy of meditation to rise throughout the body.

The seven endocrine glands act as conduits of energy between the physical body and the spiritual forces that provides each individual with life. The spiritual nature of each individual exists as a potential within every individual. It is simply waiting to be awakened by the human will. As that spiritual nature is awakened, symbols and images can be brought to mind that portray internal conflicts and struggles. These same conflicts and struggles are often depicted in legend, myth, and fairy tale because they are archetypal or universal experiences that every individual must encounter. Ultimately, the soul longs to be more fully connected to its spiritual source. The process of meditation and personal attunement can be instrumental in making that connection more fully conscious to the individual.

Conclusion

Perhaps the ultimate and most important search undertaken by each individual is the search to find one's self. For that reason, throughout all of recorded history questions such as "Who am I?" "What is the purpose of life?" and "Why am I here?" have prompted much of humankind to become seekers, seeking self-knowledge, spiritual fulfillment, and an understanding of self's relationship to the divine. This collective search has often been portrayed in stories, fairy tales, myth, and history through a variety of universal themes and symbols. To be sure, these universal patterns and symbols often remain just beyond the bounds of conscious awareness, but even there they continue to have an immeasurable influence upon each and every individual.

For example, although fairy tales such as *The Ugly Duckling* can be read simply as children's stories, they have become classics because they encapsulate something universal about the human condition and, in this case, each individual's search for his or her true self. Similarly, the warring gods of Greek and Roman myth have something to say about the divine nature of humankind and the internal struggles and warring conflicts that occur as the spiritual self finds itself in opposition to the more material side of self. Even art and architecture often contain symbolic meanings that move beyond the importance of the work or structure itself and somehow provide insights into humanity's struggles, beliefs, and ultimate destiny. For instance, the Great Pyramid at Giza might be described by some as an ancient structure for initiation or by others as simply a tomb. However, perhaps the shape itself actually symbolizes something much deeper about the nature of reality, such as the one spirit (the pyramid's apex) manifesting into the four corners of the earth.

These universal patterns of human experience are integrally connected to the subconscious mind. Because the language of the brain is ultimately symbols, working with symbols can awaken and even quicken aspects of the individual's true self that are dormant or remain just beyond personal awareness. For this reason, Edgar Cayce believed that an investigation into the subconscious should actually become "the great study for the human family." (3744-5) In this manner, the search for self could more easily be accomplished and individuals would obtain invaluable insights into themselves, their relationship to one another, and ultimately their relationship to God.

Throughout his life, Edgar Cayce recommended a variety of approaches and tools that individuals could undertake for studying these subconscious parts of the self and the deeper reaches of the human mind. Suggested approaches included such things as meditation and personal attunement, the study of dreams, working with any of the creative arts, introspection and self-evaluation, and several tools for exploring the subject of symbolism. Many of these tools essentially enabled the individual to set aside any biases and patterns existing at the level of the conscious mind and more fully access the spiritual components that resided deep within the self. Cayce believed that these types of techniques and others could be instrumental in enabling individuals to more fully know themselves. Simply stated, Cayce advised, "Study those and *know thyself.*" (3744-5) In addition to awakening spiritual awareness, exploring the inner self is an effective tool for facilitating personal wholeness and integrating disconnected components within the individual.

As a means of promoting personal growth and wholeness, three approaches were frequently recommended to individuals, each somewhat unique to the Cayce information. The suggestions were to create and utilize life seals, to create and explore what Cayce called an aura chart, and to study the Book of Revelation with the idea that the imagery being portrayed symbolically illustrated the universal pattern of awakening consciousness that occurred within each individual.

Somewhat similar to a mandala, a life seal can be described as a material representation of an important direction, a personal talent that one wishes to express more fully, a past experience, or even a soul reminder. Generally composed of only a few symbols, life seals can be used for personal motivation. Essentially, they utilize symbols to remind the individual of what he or she is trying to accomplish in life. A life seal can focus on a quality that needs to be further developed or it might also symbolize something that the individual is trying to change about himself or herself.

Edgar Cayce advised using a life seal each morning as a reminder of what an individual hoped to accomplish during the day. The seal could be reflected upon again at night as a means of contemplating the day's successes as well those experiences that could be done differently in the future. With this in mind, a life seal can be used much like a personal affirmation——awakening or somehow quickening within the individual the desire to know self, the consciousness of what she or he hopes to become, and an awareness of the individual's relationship to the divine.

Used in a similar manner, an aura chart is an oblong picture that includes symbols, pictures, and illustrations to record both the achievements and failures of the soul's journey through various lifetimes. The chart essentially draws upon those periods in history that are having the most influential affect upon the individual in the present. Edgar Cayce stated that the composition of an aura chart uses symbols to bring to mind an individual's purpose as well as soul strengths and weaknesses. It can also be helpful for getting in touch with one's highest ideals and aspirations. This awakened awareness can be instrumental in facilitating personal growth and development. As is true for life seals, aura charts can be re-created or revised whenever the individual desires to do so.

One of the most helpful tools for personal and soul growth recommended by the Cayce information, ultimately enabling the individual to come to know one's self, is meditation. Meditation allows the individual to quiet the sometimes distracting and materially minded consciousness and instead awaken the spiritual or higher self that resides deep within. Edgar Cayce believed that this awakening soul self was perhaps best depicted by John's visionary experience during meditation that became the Book of Revelation.

Rather than being associated with prophecy and external events, the Revelation is first and foremost an archetypal or universal experience that holds clues to the nature of human consciousness. Essentially, the symbolism portrays the internal struggles that occur within each individual as spiritual development takes place and the basic lower nature of humankind evolves into its higher spiritual nature. Because John's experience embodied the optimal process in which this higher self is awakened, Cayce believed that it ultimately presented an approach that was relevant for all of humankind.

The symbolism of the Revelation is best compared to the workings of the human body and evolving consciousness. For example, the images of the four beasts are integrally connected to the influences of the lower centers and the personal motivations of self-gratification, self-preservation, self-propagation, and self-sustenance. The dragon can be compared to each individual's rebellious spirit. The arrival of the New Jerusalem can be associated with the eventual supremacy of the higher self and the realization of each soul's higher purposes and desires. Just as John's spiritual centers were somehow awakened during his meditative experience and the more basic urges and desires were forced to bow down and become subservient to this higher self, all individuals can examine the symbolism of the Revelation for insights into their own attunement, growth, and development. With this in mind, rather than be associated with external events and even prophecy, the Revelation should instead be associated primarily with an internal process.

The use of symbols can be beneficial throughout life. The nature of symbolism is that it can assist each individual in understanding everything about the self: strengths and abilities, faults and weaknesses, innate desires and purposes, and ultimately even the purpose for which the individual was born. Because the subconscious mind holds clues to the uniqueness and individuality of the self, working with personal symbolism can be extremely helpful in facilitating self-awareness, personal wholeness, and soul development.

The journey of life is one of self-discovery. It is a lifelong process in which each individual has the opportunity to come to know self. It is a process of growing awareness in which each individual comes to realize that the Self is much more than he or she ever imagined. Ultimately it is an awareness of the individual's uniqueness and the soul's connection to the rest of all Creation.

Appendix A:
Edgar Cayce's Symbolism for Life Seals and Aura Charts

Note: The symbols for colors, numbers, planets, and the zodiac are arranged by category first and then alphabetically. For example, "Red" is indexed under Colors: Red; "Mercury" is indexed under Planets: Mercury; "Three" is indexed under Numbers: Three; and, "Gemini" is indexed under Zodiac: Gemini.

Altar

Corresponds to offerings. Associated with personal sacrifice. A place to display or present what is being worshipped by self or others.

Anchor	Might be symbolic of being anchored in the cross. Can be associated with personal stability. Could be representative of a depth of emotions or spirituality.
Angel	Can correspond to personal spirituality or one's ideal. Associated with wisdom, guidance or truth. Can indicate a helpful messenger or a servant of the divine.
Ankh	A symbol of life. Could be associated with an Egyptian past-life influence.
Arch	Can represent that which connects the old with the new. A bridge between worlds of thought. A doorway to understanding.
Ark	The Ark of the Covenant is symbolic of communication with the divine. Noah's Ark is representative of transformation and personal protection. Either might be associated with a past-life experience.
Armor	Can be associated with the armor of God (e.g., truth, faith). Symbolic of personal protection and defense. Might be indicative of a past-life influence or experience (e.g., the Crusades).
Arrow	Associated with that which is sent out (e.g., a message). Could correspond to intention or swiftness. Symbolic of that which hits the mark.
Athlete	Corresponds to health, strength, and personal agility. Might be associated with a past-life experience.
Atlantis	The struggle between good and evil—

the children of the Law of One and the sons of Belial. Could be associated with a past-life experience. Symbolic of technology and mechanical achievement.

Baby

Symbolic of a new beginning, a new idea or direction, or a new relationship. Can correspond with innocence and the need for direction and guidance. Associated with childlike faith and openness. That which is new or yet-to-be developed. Could indicate a literal child or children.

Balance

Associated with keeping one's life in balance. A balanced approach to the physical, mental, and spiritual aspects of life. Might indicate a balance of truth.

Ball

Can correspond to wholeness, completeness or oneness. Associated with a well-rounded approach to things. Can be indicative of games or joyfulness.

Banyan Tree

Associated with spirituality, especially Buddhist thought. Might be indicative of a past-life experience.

Battle Ax

Associated with a warrior of truth or of earthly conflict. Can be symbolic of a past-life experience.

Beach

Can be symbolic of the sands of time. Might correspond to the joining of the spiritual and material worlds. Could be associated with a past-life experience.

Bear

Can correspond to anger and aggression. Might be symbolic of one whom is able to bear or endure. Associated with what one thinks of bears. Culturally, may be indicative of that which is failing or falling (e.g., a bear market).

Bee/Honey Bee

Associated with personal activity and the cycle of life. Can be representative of the activity and industriousness of the individual, body, mind, or spirit (e.g., a busy bee). A honeybee can symbolize cooperation and industriousness (e.g., one who is cooperative for the good of the whole). A bee can be associated with being flighty, mean, or unproductive.

Bell

A calling; a message or an announcement. That which may send out warnings or messages of aid and help to others.

Berries

Symbolic of creative energies and talents. Might be associated with fruits of the spirit or talents.

Bible

Corresponds to spiritual truths, insight, and wisdom. Could be symbolic of a past-life experience (e.g., the era of the Old and New Testaments). See Book.

Bird

Associated with a message. Can be symbolic of freedom from the material world. Might be representative of the spirit, spiritual knowledge, or the higher self. Can correspond to thoughts, aspirations, and ideals. The type of bird generally is important to the message being relayed (e.g., a dove can be associated with love, a rooster with the dawn of a new day, a sparrow with the arrival of spring, etc.).

Bird of Paradise

Associated with peace and harmony. Can indicate achievements or things that are

	desired to be personally acquired.
Blood	Symbolic of the life force and energy. Could be associated with personal sacrifice. Can represent the sacrifice of the Christ.
Blossoms/Buds	May indicate talents and abilities. Associated with growth and personal expression. Symbolic of expectancy or a new beginning. That which springs forth to life.
Boat	Often associated with a spiritual journey. Can be symbolic of an emotional experience. Could correspond to the journey of life. Indicative of the unconscious. Might be related to a new beginning, opportunity, or experience.
Book	Associated with knowledge and wisdom. May indicate the Akashic Records, the Book of Life, soul memory (e.g., life's experiences), the Bible, or other scriptures. Can correspond to lessons and ideas. Could be symbolic of latent knowledge and abilities. A life journey/experience that has yet to be written or lived. A personal search.
Book of Life	Representative of the soul's journey, the Akashic Records, and God's book of remembrance.
Bouquet	Can be symbolic of one's talents and abilities. Associated with the beauty of a life well lived.
Branches	That which reaches out to others. May correspond to the tree of life.

Bread	Often associated with the bread of life. A source of supply for body, mind, or spirit. Give us this day our daily bread. The staff of life. That which permits development at all levels. Might be symbolic of money or financial rewards.
Bricks	Can correspond to that which is created one element at a time (e.g., "line upon line, precept upon precept"). Could be symbolic of stability.
Bridge	That which leads to a new direction. Associated with a connection. Can correspond to the bridge between understanding and ignorance. Might be symbolic of a transition.
Bull	Can be associated with hardheadedness or stubbornness. Symbolic of the first chakra or spiritual center. Could indicate sexuality. Culturally, may be representative of growth or prosperity (e.g., a bull market).
Bull's-Eye	Might be associated with ideals or aspirations. Could indicate personal attunement. One who hits the mark.
Bush with buds	Associated with new growth and possibilities. Could be associated with talents or abilities. Corresponds to expectancy. Leaves, blossoms, and buds are all symbolic of life.
Butterfly	Can correspond to personal or spiritual transformation. Symbolic of a personal awakening. Might be associated with freedom or taking flight.

Camel	Associated with Egypt and the desert. Could correspond to a past-life experience. May be symbolic of a journey of hardship. Might represent a bearer of water (e.g., spiritual, emotional, or physical sustenance).
Candle/Candelabra	That which is a light to the world. A candle can be symbolic of wisdom, enlightenment, or singleness of purpose. The candelabra can correspond to the seven spiritual centers of the body. See Menorah.
Captain	One who is in charge of a (spiritual) journey. Can represent a source of guidance, authority, power, or direction. Might be associated with the higher self.
Car	Often symbolic of one's life's direction. That which travels the journey of life. Depending upon the car's appearance, may indicate that which is sleek, material, out of control, or a wreck.
Caravan	Associated with the ancient past or a past-life experience (Persia, Egypt, etc.) Can correspond to the desert.
Carpenter	The Christ. Might be symbolic of the act of creativity or building something. Could represent a past-life experience.
Cat	Most often symbolic of whatever an individual associates with cats. Could be symbolic of independence or playfulness.
Chain Links	A symbol of connectedness. That which holds, binds, aids, or follows another.

	Could indicate cooperation and team-work.
Chalice/Cup	Symbolic of one's life mission or purpose. Might be associated with soul memory or karma. May correspond to the Christ.
Chariot (with Horses)	May be associated with modes of travel or communication. Could indicate a past-life experience in Greece or Rome.
Charm (Jewelry)	Can symbolize a protective influence. That which aids and assists.
Cherub	An angelic influence. Associated with spirituality. Could indicate a divine messenger.
Child/Children	Can be associated with a new beginning or direction. Can be symbolic of innocence, hope, or simplicity. An undeveloped potential. Could correspond to working with children, being helpful to children, one's desire for children, or the biblical "receive the kingdom of God as a little child." (Mark 10:15)
Christ	Corresponds to spirituality and unconditional love. The ultimate Ideal. One's Master or Elder brother. A divine messenger. Could be associated with a past-life experience at the time of Jesus.
Church	Associated with spirituality. Could be indicative of spiritual community. May be symbolic of the safety and security of spiritual forces. One's religious beliefs. Might represent the highest ideal or the ultimate self.

Circle	Associated with wholeness and the inner self. Can be symbolic of oneness or completeness. Might correspond with "the Lord thy God is One." That which is all encompassing or eternal.
Cliffs	Could indicate a challenging experience or goal. Might be symbolic of rough treading or the possibility of danger. May be associated with a past-life locale.
Cloud	Associated with the divine or that which is heavenly. Could be symbolic of one's wishes or dreams. Might indicate confusion.
Clover	Corresponds to growth, greenery, and nature. A four-leaf clover may be symbolic of good luck and prosperity.
Coat of Arms	Represents a family group or heritage. That from which one comes. Symbolic of genealogy and heraldry.
Colors	Variations in colors can correspond to caution, changing circumstance, or transformation.
Colors: Black	Can correspond to the unknown, the unconscious, or the mysterious. Could indicate the need for cleansing. Might be indicative of fear or the end of something.
Colors: Blue	Generally associated with spirituality. Corresponds to religious or spiritual truth, calm, and higher levels of healing. The color of the sky and the heavenly realms. Dark blue may indicate spiritual awakening.

Colors: Brown	Can be associated with the earth, being grounded, and practicality. Might be symbolic of materialism or earthiness.
Colors: Coral	May indicate material-mindedness (e.g., that which is beautiful but potentially dangerous). Could be symbolic of talents or abilities.
Colors: Gold	Associated with spiritual truths. That which is valuable and incorruptible. Could correspond to powers of the soul. Might indicate personal attainment.
Colors: Gray	Can be associated with moodiness, discouragement, or sadness. May be symbolic of the mysterious.
Colors: Green	Often corresponds to healing. Can be associated with nature, growth, and development. Could be symbolic of envy (e.g., being green with envy).
Colors: Indigo	Associated with the higher self. Might be symbolic of the Christ energy.
Colors: Orange	Can be associated with either creativity or sexuality. Might be symbolic of the sun, energy, or power.
Colors: Pink	Symbolic of the emotions. Might indicate the influence of love. Metaphorically, "in the pink" is representative of good health.
Colors: Purple	Can correspond to high-mindedness or high mental abilities. Symbolic of royalty. Could indicate higher vibrations. Might represent spiritual healing.
Colors: Red	Associated with energy, force, passion,

	and vigor. Can be indicative of a temper or anger. Can be symbolic of blood. Might represent the color of danger (e.g., a stop sign).
Colors: Rose	Associated with beauty, love and the manifestation of nature.
Colors: Silver	That which is valuable or holy. Could be associated with higher levels of consciousness.
Colors: Violet	The highest level of spiritual attainment. Might correlate to the divine or oneness. Associated with an attitude of seeking.
Colors: White	Can be indicative of purity, innocence, holiness, and perfection. The white light is associated with the divine. Can correspond to wholeness and the complete integration of all colors of the spectrum. The ultimate ideal. May be associated with selfless service.
Colors: Yellow	Generally corresponds to the energy of thoughts and ideas. Might correlate to energy of personal power.
Columns (Building)	Associated with the past or a possible past-life experience (e.g., Rome, Greece, Egypt, Persia and Atlantis). That which provides stability.
Compass	Corresponds to one's personal direction in life. Associated with a source of guidance. May also be suggestive of a goal or an ideal.
Coral	Could indicate talents and abilities. Symbolic of spirituality manifesting in the

material world. Could represent emotions or creativity. May be associated with self-expression. Might correspond to material-mindedness.

Corn

A source of supply and bounty. Symbolic of the harvest. Might be associated with a past-life experience (e.g., farmer, Indian, etc.).

Cornucopia/ Horn of Plenty

Can be associated with prosperity in material, emotional, or spiritual things. Can be symbolic of the source of supply. May indicate personal abundance. Might symbolize that which pours forth onto others.

Crockery/Pots

Associated with trade and the marketplace. Could represent a personal past-life experience (e.g., as a member of a caravan).

Cross

Associated with the Christ. Can indicate personal sacrifice or crucifixion. Represents the ultimate ideal, guiding force, or influence. The bridge between the spirit and materiality. Can correspond to personal crosses to bear. Mastery over the earth. Might symbolize spiritual truths.

Cross and the Crown

Corresponds to the Christ. Associated with spiritual lessons, hardship and personal transformation. Can be indicative of overcoming the things of the earth.

Crown

Can represent royalty, wisdom, or authority. Could correspond to spiritual attainment. A crown of thorns is symbolic of the Christ, personal sacrifice, or hardship.

Crystal	May be symbolic of spiritual insight or wisdom. That which becomes valuable by undergoing hardship. Might correspond to Atlantis.
Crystal (Atlantean)	May be associated with technology, the misuse of power, or a past-life experience in Atlantis.
Dance/Dancers/ Dancing	May correspond to the dance of life (e.g., life's journey). Can be associated with movement and fluidity. Might be symbolic of a past-life experience.
Dancing Girl	Associated with joy and exuberance. Can correspond to temple services from the ancient past. Freedom and personal expression. Might correspond to a dance hall.
Dawn	Can indicate a new beginning or the awakening of something new. Symbolic of a fresh approach or insight. Might correspond to healing, faith, or a new understanding.
Diamond	Often corresponds to a relationship. Can be associated with eternity, truth, love, or something of great value. That which has been transformed through hardship.
Disc with Javelin	Associated with a past-life experience. Can correspond to mastery of the physical world.
Dog	Most often symbolic of whatever one associates with dogs. Culturally, representative of friendship and faithfulness. Might indicate trustworthiness, instinct, or obedience. That which can be both

	friendly and aggressive. Might be a metaphor for "going to the dogs" or going badly.
Donkey	May correspond to stubbornness, humility, the Christ, or hope. Could represent that which is a heavy load.
Door/Doorway	Can represent a new beginning, opportunity, or direction. Might be indicative of the pathway to the inner self. Symbolic of the open door between self and the divine.
Dove	Can correspond to the spiritual realms. A messenger of peace or love. Might represent the Holy Spirit.
Dragon	Can be symbolic of evil or selfishness. Might indicate fear. May represent the power of the unconscious. Could be representative of the rebellious spirit.
Drum	May correspond to one's direction or life path (e.g., following the beat of a drum). Could be symbolic of the rhythms in life or a heartbeat. Metaphorically, beating the drum is associated with presenting a personal viewpoint.
Dynamite	Can be symbolic of explosive emotions or a temper. Might correspond to an explosive power. Could indicate a powerful force.
Eagle	Associated with vision, power, and freedom. May be symbolic of strength, insight, or spiritual heights. Might correspond to the United States. Symbolic of the fourth chakra or spiritual center.

Ear	Associated with a good listener. Can indicate compassion or a counseling ability.
EL	Name used by Edgar Cayce to suggest God or the presence of the divine. Might correspond to Elohim (God) or El Shaddai (God Almighty).
Electricity	That which is charged or energized. The source of power (e.g., spirituality). Might represent enlightenment. The act of being empowered.
Elephant	Often symbolic of memory. Might correspond to wisdom and enlightenment. Associated with power, strength and might. Could be representative of one who is "thick skinned."
Emerald	Associated with healing and enlightenment. That which has become valuable by undergoing hardship.
Eucharist	Can symbolize the Christ influence. Might be associated with the Church.
Eye (All-Seeing)	Can be associated with spiritual vision or the divine. Corresponds to singleness of purpose, ideals, and awakening consciousness. Can indicate clairvoyance, vision, or one's outlook. Could be representative of the self or self-reflection. Might be symbolic of the oneness of all life.
Feathers	Can correspond to thoughts and ideas. May be associated with the heavenly realms and aspirations.

Feet/Footprints	Corresponds to one's personal life path. May be symbolic of stability, personal understanding, grounding, or a new direction.
Fence	Symbolic of any kind of enclosure, limit, barrier, or protection.
Fern	May correspond to nature, growth, and creation. Might represent the mysterious.
Field	Associated with possibilities. Can correspond to one's surroundings and present experience.
Fire	Can be associated with transformation and change. Might be symbolic of anger, rage, or evil. Could represent energy and activity. Corresponds with a "trial by fire." Can represent passion, sexuality, or bodily fevers.
Fireworks	Associated with celebration and achievement. Could represent creativity and inner expression. Might correspond to public acclaim and recognition.
Fish	Can be symbolic of spirituality or the Christ. A representative of the Piscean Age. Could correspond to a past-life experience in Palestine. Might indicate that which can be drawn out or attained.
Flag	Corresponds to movements, groups, or belief systems. Often associated with nationalities. Might indicate an ideal or the call to something greater than self.

Fleur de Lis	Former French family royal symbol. Can be symbolic of honor, diplomacy, strength, might, or power. Associated with a reverence to duty toward others. Represents freedom and yet the dependence of one upon another. Could correspond to a past-life experience.
Flowers	The expression of inner talents and creativity. Can be symbolic of beauty, innocence, growth, and glory. Associated with expectancy or one's unfolding life experience. That in life which is about to blossom or bloom.
Flying	May correspond to hopes, dreams, aspirations, or spirituality. Could represent soaring above the material plane. Might symbolize desires or wishes. A mode of travel.
Forest	Associated with peace, growth, contemplation, thoughts and ideas, creation, darkness, or chaos. Could indicate the unconscious mind. Might represent a particular locale or a past-life experience.
Fountain	Can symbolize the source of supply or the water of life. Associated with spirit or emotions. Might represent a particular locale or a past-life experience.
Fruit	The fruits of the spirit. That which sustains life. A fruitful life. Could symbolize one's talents or abilities.
G	The letter "G" can be associated with God, Jehovah, or the presence of the divine.

Gate	Can correspond to a new possibility. Might be associated with a barrier between two worlds.
Golden Calf	May indicate a past-life influence at the time of Moses. Corresponds to ancient Egypt. Can be associated with material things, idolatry, or the worship of the lower self (e.g., the bull is the symbol for the first chakra at the level of the gonads).
Grass	Symbolic of the life force, nature, growth, and greenery. That which springs to life or seeks the light.
Greenery	May represent health and healing, nature, growth, or development.
Hammer	Corresponds to personal labors or building. The driving force in a situation. Might symbolize the desire to have power or personal control.
Hammer and Sickle	Symbolic of reaping and sowing and the efforts of one's personal labors. A hammer might be associated with building or labors and a sickle might correspond to death.
Hammock	Could correspond to relaxation, harmony, inner reflection, or idleness.
Handmaiden/Maid	May be symbolic of a handmaiden of the Lord. Could correspond to service. Might represent a past-life experience.
Hands	Often symbolic of the self, self's abilities, or talents. Associated with what an individual possesses within self. Inter-

locking hands can be symbolic of cooperation, community, and fellowship. A hand reaching out can represent the act of giving out to others in service.

Harp

Associated with harmony. Corresponds to musical tendencies and abilities. Might correspond to a past-life influence. Could indicate initiation or the music of the heavenly realms.

Hat

May be symbolic of thoughts and ideas or one's personal profession.

Heart

Associated with love. Can indicate whole-heartedness. One who is true hearted. Might correspond to passion or a weakness of the flesh.

Helmet

The protection of thoughts and ideas. A warrior for the divine. May indicate a period of conflict or physical power. Could correspond to a personal past-life experience.

Hemlock

Associated with poison. Might symbolize the act of poisoning one's self or being poisoned.

Hieroglyphics

Associated with ancient Egypt. May symbolize the expression of thoughts and ideas. Could correspond to a past-life experience.

Historical Epochs

May be symbolic of past-life influences or experiences (e.g., Atlantean, Egyptian, Persian, Palestinian, during the Crusades, European, early American, etc.)

Holly

Can be symbolic of nature, the spirit of

	Christmas, personal trials, or temptation.
Holy Women	Can be indicative of a past-life experience. Associated with Jesus. May be symbolic of love, service, and spirituality. Could correspond to healing abilities.
Home/House	Associated with the importance of home and family. Could symbolize the heavenly home. Can correspond to the desire for harmony in one's personal surroundings.
Honey Bee/Bee	Associated with personal activity and the cycle of life. Can be representative of the activity and industriousness of the individual, body, mind, or spirit (e.g., a busy bee). A honeybee can symbolize cooperation and industriousness (e.g., one who is cooperative for the good of the whole). A bee can be associated with being flighty, mean, or unproductive.
Horn of Plenty/ Cornucopia	Can be associated with prosperity in material, emotional, or spiritual things. Can be symbolic of the source of supply. May indicate personal abundance. Might symbolize that which pours forth onto others.
Horse	A messenger for the body, the mind, or the spirit. Can be symbolic of change. Could correspond to instincts, freedom, or something that is unbridled.
Hourglass	Symbolic of the sands of time. May represent opportunities to come as well as those which have passed.

Ibex Bird	Associated with ancient Egypt and royalty. Can correspond to higher spiritual development. May be symbolic of a past-life experience in Egypt.
Jesus	Corresponds to spirituality and unconditional love. The ultimate Ideal. One's Master or Elder brother. A divine messenger. Could be associated with a past-life experience at the time of Jesus.
Jewelry	Often symbolic of talents and abilities. Could be associated with spiritual insight. Might indicate material prosperity.
Key	Symbolic of a key to understanding. That which opens the inner self. A new beginning. Can be indicative of personal security, a personal search, or the answers for which one has been seeking.
King	May represent one's higher self or God. Associated with higher thoughts and ideas. A ruling influence. Could correspond to a past-life experience.
Ladder	Can correspond to higher states of consciousness, success, or personal attainment. May be associated with one's life path, one step at a time.
Lake	Can indicate peace and tranquility, contemplation, or reflection. Might symbolize a particular locale or a past-life experience.
Lamb	Associated with purity, the lamb of God and the Christ. Could correspond to a past-life experience.

Lapis Lazuli	Can symbolize strength, vitality, self-assurance and intuition. That which has become valuable through hardship.
Last Supper	Associated with the Christ. Can correspond to a past-life experience.
Leaves	Can be symbolic of nature, growth, or thoughts and ideas.
Left	May be symbolic of the past, being liberal, and the feminine. Metaphorically, being left-brained can indicate logic and intellect.
Light	Can correspond to the divine. Associated with the light of truth, the light of the world, or great insight. That which lights one's way. Symbolic of spirit entering into the earth. Might represent love, peace, understanding, or happiness. Can indicate higher consciousness.
Lightning	Associated with power, insight, or an emotional outburst. Could symbolize the higher forces or the divine. Might represent mysticism or instant karma.
Lilies	Can be associated with spiritual development, rebirth, and resurrection. Symbolic of beauty and purity. Might correspond to the Christ energy.
Lion	Can represent strength, royalty, or personal power. Could be associated with courage. Symbolic of the third chakra or spiritual center.
Log	Associated with strength, stability, or nature.

Lotus	May symbolize enlightenment, beauty, or innocence. Can represent spirituality coming forth from the earth. Might be a symbol for being in the earth but not of the earth (e.g., it often blooms atop dirty water).
Maid/Handmaiden	May be symbolic of a handmaiden of the Lord. Could correspond to service. Might represent a past-life experience.
Meditator	Associated with relaxation, inner peace, and enlightenment. Might indicate oneness and at-onement.
Menorah	Associated with light. Can correspond to spiritual truths and illumination. May represent the spiritual centers. Might be symbolic of a past-life experience. See Candle/Candelabra.
Money	Associated with wealth, prosperity, personal influence, and materiality.
Monk	Associated with spirituality and one's higher self. Could indicate a spiritual presence. Might be symbolic of a past-life experience.
Moon ☾	Symbolic of emotions, romance, sentimentality, intuition, and the unconscious. Can correspond to change, cycles, or the passage of time. Often associated with a feminine influence. Can indicate receptivity, feelings, or desire.
Mortise and Tenon	Could be associated with cooperation. Might be symbolic of virtue and understanding.

Mountain	Can correspond to higher states of consciousness. Could indicate a challenge or a destiny. Associated with enlightenment, attainment, or one's personal ambitions. A sacred place. May correspond to the mount. Might be associated with a past-life locale.
Mt. Horeb	Associated with the burning bush, the past, Moses, and God's covenant. Could correspond to strength.
Mt. of Olives	Associated with the life and work of Jesus. Could correspond to a past-life experience.
Mt. Sinai	Corresponds to Moses and the Ten Commandments.
Music	Can symbolize the music of the spheres and harmony. Could represent a personal talent or ability.
National Emblems	Associated with groups and masses, a national identity, or a group consciousness. May be representative of a past-life experience as a member of that group or ideology. See Flag.
Neck	Symbolic of the will and the self. Might correspond to one who is "stiff-necked."
Number of Objects	Can correspond to a like number of talents, things, concerns, experiences, children, etc. Might indicate a period or time (e.g., days, months, years, etc.).
Numbers: 1	Corresponds to the beginning. The essence of all that exists or emanates from the One. Might indicate the Lord thy God

is ONE. The energy of the first chakra.

Numbers: 2

Associated with the creative principle. May correspond to companionship. Can be related to divisiveness and weakness or cooperation, union, and strength. The energy of the second chakra.

Numbers: 3

Can be symbolic of the triune nature of God. May correspond to the body, the mind and the spirit. Associated with the three phases of human experience: physical, mental, and spiritual. The energy of the third chakra.

Numbers: 4

Corresponds to the material plane, stability, and order. Might indicate the four seasons or the four elements. The energy of the fourth chakra.

Numbers: 5

Can be symbolic of change or the five senses. The energy of the fifth chakra.

Numbers: 6

Associated with beauty, harmony, and symmetry. The energy of the sixth chakra.

Numbers: 7

Can represent the spiritual forces. A sacred number. Indicative of the seven spiritual centers/chakras or endocrine glands or the energy of the seventh chakra. Might represent spiritual perfection.

Numbers: 8

Can be associated with either being combined in strength or combined in weakness. Might indicate balance, attainment, or infinity.

Numbers: 9

Can be symbolic of wholeness, completeness, or fulfillment. Could correspond to an imminent change.

Numbers: 10	Associated with strength or a completeness in numbers.
Numbers: 11	Can correspond to power, beauty, or betrayal. Can be symbolic of physical perfection.
Numbers: 12	Associated with ritual, mysticism, and cosmic order. Could be associated with the Apostles, the months of the year, or the twelve tribes of Israel.
Numbers: 22	Can correspond to personal fulfillment. Can be symbolic of mental perfection.
Numbers: 33	Associated with the Christ. Can be symbolic of spiritual perfection.
Nun	Associated with spirituality and one's higher self. Could indicate a spiritual presence. Might be symbolic of a past-life experience.
Nurse	Can correspond to a healing influence or one who is a healer.
Oasis	A place of refuge and safety. Might correspond to a geographical locale or a past-life experience.
Ocean	Associated with spirit or the emotions. Can correspond to a spiritual or emotional journey. Might indicate the unconscious mind. Associated with water and the source of all that exists in the earth. Can correspond to feelings, moods, or desires. May be symbolic of the feminine.
Ohm	Symbolic of God the Creator/Father/Mother and the divine presence. Can

correspond to a goal or a divine ideal. Associated with the highest influence and vibration possible. Can represent the physical or heavenly home. Might indicate oneness as in "the Lord thy God is One." The building block of the universe. The sound of the word can also be representative of the "home."

Old Man/Old Woman

Could represent wisdom through experience. One who is a seer or sage. Might symbolize the keeper of the Akashic Records or soul memory.

Olive Branch

Associated with peace. Could indicate the Christ influence.

Owl

Associated with wisdom. One who is clear-seeing. Might indicate a messenger of knowledge or information.

Paper/Parchment

Can correspond to one who is a scribe or a communicator. May be associated with the soul's record, the Book of Life, or Akashic Record.

Papyrus

Associated with Egypt, communication, and keeping a record. May correspond to a past-life experience.

Path

One's journey and direction in life. Could correspond to a new beginning.

Pearl

Often symbolic of that attained through hardship and personal sacrifice (e.g., a pearl of great price). May be indicative of wisdom or purity. That which comes into being through stress.

Pen

Associated with writing or communication. Could indicate a personal commitment or agreement.

Pig

May symbolize whatever one thinks of pigs. Might indicate casting away that which is of the lower self.

Planets

Can correspond to the developmental stages of the soul. Associated with phases of one's personal consciousness.

Planets: Earth

Associated with materiality, third-dimensional consciousness, the flesh, or a descent from the spiritual realm. Can correspond to other places, other cultures, other people, and other lands. Might be symbolic of the whole.

Planets: Jupiter

Often associated with broadness of vision. Can symbolize strength, large ideas, and nobleness of purpose. Might indicate universality.

Planets: Mars

Often associated with action, power, a pioneering spirit, and creative energy. Might correspond to one who defends others. Can symbolize anger, aggressiveness, or one who possesses a temper or is prone to warlike behavior.

Planets: Mercury

Often associated with mental influences, the mind, or wisdom. Can symbolize personal seeking, high mental abilities, and one who is prone to judgment. Might suggest the influence of personal meditation.

Planets: Moon

See Moon.

Planets: Neptune

Often associated with mysticism, spiritual insights, and clairvoyance. Can symbolize the mysterious.

Planets: Pluto ♇
(Vulcan/Septimus)

Associated with consciousness, transformation, and regeneration. Can symbolize self-centeredness or the potential for spiritual growth.

Planets: Saturn ♄

Associated with new beginnings, sudden change, or rebirth. Might be associated with self-discipline and patience. Can symbolize earthly woes or periods of personal testing.

Planets: Sun

See Sun.

Planets: Uranus ♅

Associated with the psychic, intuition, and insight. Can symbolize the unusual or the tendency of going to extremes. Might indicate independence.

Planets: Venus ♀

Associated with love and an appreciation for beauty. Can symbolize femininity, music, or the emotions. Might correspond to a friendly disposition and being adept in the social arts.

Police

Could indicate one's higher self. May be symbolic of spiritual or karmic law. Might represent the protective forces.

Priest

Associated with spirituality and one's higher self. Could indicate a spiritual presence. Might be symbolic of a past-life experience.

Prism

That which diffuses color in materiality. Can correspond to the integration of the whole (the seven centers).

Pyramid

May correspond to personal initiation

and transformation. Associated with spirituality, mysticism, and psychic ability. An inverted pyramid can be symbolic of spirit entering into materiality. Might be associated with ancient teachings. Could correspond to a past-life experience.

Question Mark—?

Associated with the unknown. The act of questioning the rationale as to whether something was undertaken for the spirit, the mind, or the body. Can symbolize a period of questioning or the need to ask questions.

Rain

Can correspond to the emotions or the release of feelings. Could indicate a cleansing process. Might be associated with spirituality.

Rainbow

Can be indicative of prosperity. Might symbolize the seven spiritual centers or wholeness. Associated with a covenant or a promise. That which is of the divine. Corresponds to the seven colors of the rainbow (red, orange, yellow, green, blue, indigo, and violet). Could indicate awakening consciousness.

Ram

Most often symbolic of whatever an individual associates with rams. Could be symbolic of courage, strength, or sacrifice. Might be indicative of an Egyptian past-life experience (e.g., Khnum is the ram-headed Egyptian god of creation).

Right

May be symbolic of the future, being conservative, and the masculine. Metaphorically, being right-brained can

	indicate intuition and receptivity.
Ring	Often associated with an obligation, a relationship, a goal, or an achievement. Can correspond to wholeness or one-ness.
River	May represent a spiritual journey or the passage of time. That which divides.
Road/Street	One's journey and direction in life. Could correspond to a new beginning.
Rocks	Often symbolic of challenging conditions, obstacles, or emotionally impenetrable. Might represent stability or strength.
Roof	May correspond to thoughts or ideas. Symbolic of one's understanding. Can represent protection, security, or shelter.
Rooster	Can correspond to the dawn of a new day. Could indicate one's male nature, an attitude of "cockiness," or arrogance. Might symbolize the denial of the Christ (e.g., Luke 22).
Rose	Associated with love and beauty. Might be symbolic of a relationship. Can represent patience, faith, and the sweetness of life.
Rose of Sharon	Biblically, associated with love and devotion (e.g., Song of Solomon 2:1).
Ruby	Can correspond to love and compassion.
Runner	Might indicate a strong impetus on one's life journey. The need or desire to reach one's goal. Might symbolize a messenger.

Sailing Ship	Often associated with a spiritual or emotional journey. Could indicate travel or the imagination. Might represent a past-life experience.
Scales	Associated with decision-making, balance, and justice.
Scarab	An Egyptian beetle. Associated with good luck and prosperity. May be symbolic of a past-life experience or influence.
School	Can correspond to higher learning or one's personal lessons in life. Might indicate the ability to teach or provide wisdom and information to others.
Scissors	Could represent the desire to cut loose from something. Might symbolize the act of removing something from one's life.
Scorpion	May correspond to that which is dangerous, poisonous, or stinging. Could indicate personal power and protection. Connected to whatever one associates with scorpions.
Scroll	Associated with one's record, the Book of Life, or the Akashic Records. Can correspond to wisdom or information. May represent one who is a scribe or a communicator. Might symbolize history.
Scythe	Often symbolic of one who is a worker in the vineyard of God. May represent the harvest or activities that can bring spiritual bounty into the material world.
Sea	Associated with spirit or the emotions.

Can correspond to a spiritual or emotional journey. Might indicate the unconscious mind. Associated with water and the source of all that exists in the earth. Can correspond to feelings, moods, or desires. May be symbolic of the feminine.

Seed/Seeds

Can indicate new beginnings or new potentials. May correspond to the seeds of truth or spiritual qualities and traits (e.g., love, patience, long-suffering, gentleness, kindness, and brotherly love). Associated with one who sows.

Seer/Seeress

Associated with intuition and wisdom. Might be indicative of a past-life experience.

Servant

Can represent the act or the need to be of service. May indicate one who is a servant for the divine. Might correspond to a past-life experience.

Sheaves

Often symbolic of one who is a worker in the vineyard of God. May represent the harvest or activities that can bring spiritual bounty into the material world. Might be associated with the passage of time.

Shells

May be associated with the sea and spirituality. Could correspond to bringing spirit into the earth. May symbolize one's talents and abilities. Might indicate the ability to turn within and listen.

Shepherd

Often symbolic of the Christ and spirituality. One who leads or nurtures a group. Might correspond to a past-life experience.

Shepherd's Rod	Symbolic of the Christ. May be associated with love through the centuries. Could indicate leadership or balance in the material experience. Might represent a spiritual journey.
Shield	Could symbolize personal protection, honor, or one's beliefs. May correspond to a past-life experience.
Ship	Often associated with a spiritual journey. Can be symbolic of an emotional experience. Could correspond to the journey of life. Indicative of the unconscious. Might be related to a new beginning, opportunity, or experience.
Shoes	Corresponds to one's personal life path. May be symbolic of stability, personal understanding, grounding, or a new direction.
Shrine	Symbolic of a place of worship. May correspond to a memorial or a reminder. Could indicate a specific locale or a past-life experience.
Sickle	Corresponds to the harvest. May be symbolic of a spiritual worker in the Lord's vineyard. Associated with sowing and reaping. Could correspond to a past-life experience.
Silhouette	Associated with the shadow of things. Could correspond to a memory or a pattern.
Snake	Often associated with sexuality, the kundalini, healing, or temptation.

Sphinx

Associated with the mysteries of Egypt. May represent ancient teachings, spiritual knowledge, or transformation. Could correspond to a past-life experience.

Spider

May be symbolic of whatever one thinks of spiders. Might represent a web of deceit.

Square

Associated with boundaries, firm parameters, or protection. Could be symbolic of balance, control, stability, or one who is emotionally controlled. Might represent "a square shooter."

Staff

Can represent the staff of life. Might correspond to a sign of authority or leadership. Could represent the Good Shepherd (e.g., the Christ). Might symbolize faith.

Stair

Can correspond to higher states of consciousness, success, or personal attainment. May be associated with one's life path, one step at a time.

Star of David

Associated with Judaism and a spiritual community. Could correspond to past-life experience.

Stars

Often corresponds to ideals, guiding influences, or attainments. Associated with guiding light and direction. That which provides a light to others. Can represent a divine influence. The Christmas star is associated with the birth of the Christ Consciousness in the material world. A five-pointed star can symbolize humanity, the five senses, or attainment through

	personal activity. A six-pointed star can symbolize love. A seven-pointed star can symbolize spiritual perfection or attainments within the seven centers of the body. An eight-pointed star can symbolize attainment.
Statue	May be associated with an emblem, a culture, or the spirit of a nation (e.g., the Statue of Liberty is associated with the U.S. and freedom, etc.).
Sun ☉	Associated with the light of spirit and the divine. May be symbolic of the Creative Force. Can correspond to righteousness, strength, or life. That which radiates out to others. Could represent hopefulness or direction. The source of supply. Might represent God's outpouring love to all of Creation.
Sunrise	Can indicate a new beginning or the awakening of something new. Symbolic of a fresh approach or insight. Might correspond to healing, faith, or a new understanding.
Sunset	Can indicate the end of something, a period of reflection, or a transition or change.
Swan	Often associated with peace and serenity. Might indicate relaxation or idleness.
Swim/Swimming	Can correspond to a spiritual or emotional experience. Might be associated with being submerged, overwhelmed, or buoyed up.
Sword	Could symbolize the sword of truth. May

represent a warrior for the divine. Could indicate that which cuts both ways. May correspond to power, authority, or aggression. Can be symbolic of male energy. Might be associated with a past-life experience.

Tadpole	Can symbolize a new beginning. Might be associated with a spiritual journey.
Teacher	Can correspond to higher learning or one's personal lessons in life. May indicate the ability to teach or provide wisdom and information to others. Might correspond to a past-life experience. Could represent a spiritual teacher or influence.
Teeth	Often associated with spoken words and communication. Might symbolize dietary habits.
Telescope	Could represent the ability to perceive with clarity. May be associated with insight and wisdom.
Temples/Temple Beautiful/Temple of Sacrifice	Can correspond to healing, transformation, and personal initiation. Symbolic of ancient mysteries or cultures. Could represent a past-life experience.
Tent/Tents	Associated with different periods in history (e.g., Native American, the nomadic tribes of the desert, etc.) and a possible past-life experience. A temporary dwelling place.
Torch/Torchbearer	Associated with truth or understanding. Could represent one who guides or lights the way of another.

Train	Can correspond to a personal journey or direction. Could be associated with a structured or destined journey. May be symbolic of being "on track." Might indicate a past-life experience (e.g., late nineteenth of early twentieth century).
Tree	Can symbolize the Tree of Life. Can represent the growth of body, mind, or spirit. Associated with strength and might.
Tree in Bloom	May represent expectancy or the blossoming of one's talents and abilities.
Triangle	Could correspond to the spiritual trinity or the body-mind-spirit. May be associated with transformation. Might represent balance (e.g., three equal sides).
Turban	May represent ancient teachings or the mysteries of the mind. Could correspond to a past-life experience.
Turtle	May be associated with longevity. Often corresponds to whatever an individual associates with turtles (e.g., slow and methodical or withdrawing into its shell—introverted).
Unicorn	May be symbolic of innocence, purity, and spirituality. Could be associated with mysticism.
Uniform	Often corresponds to duty. May represent power and authority. Could be associated with a past-life experience (e.g., a Confederate uniform, etc.). Might correspond to the spirit or beliefs of a nation.
V	The letter "V" can be associated with "V

is for victory" or it might indicate the symbol for peace.

Vine

May be symbolic of that which encircles self. Could correspond to preservation and protection. That which binds, clings to, or encircles.

Virgin Mary

Associated with a spiritual presence or the divine mother. Could correspond to a past-life experience at the time of Mary. Might indicate one's personal ideal.

Wall

Can be associated with confinement or protection. Might be symbolic of an obstacle to be overcome. Could indicate a separation. Metaphorically, represents being "up against a wall." Historical walls could represent a past-life experience (e.g., the Wall of China).

Water

Associated with spirit or the emotions. Can correspond to a spiritual or emotional journey. Might indicate the unconscious mind. The source of all life. Can correspond to feelings, moods, or desires. May be symbolic of the feminine.

Weeds

Can be associated with neglect or that which chokes out desired growth. Might indicate a period of personal hardship.

Wheat

Can be symbolic of a spiritual, mental, or physical harvest. Associated with laborers in the field of life. Might represent the bread of life. May indicate abundance. Could correspond to a past-life experience as a peasant or a farmer.

Wheel

Often associated with the wheel of life.

That which steers one's life direction. Can correspond to one who is mechanically-minded. A wheel with spokes might be representative of cooperation. Might be associated with a past-life experience.

Wine and Loaf

Can be symbolic of sustenance for the soul. Often associated with the Last Supper and the body and blood of Christ. May represent a spiritual commitment/ promise. Could correspond to a past-life experience in Palestine.

Woods

Associated with peace, growth, contemplation, thoughts and ideas, creation, darkness, or chaos. Could indicate the unconscious mind. Might represent a particular locale or a past-life experience.

Words

Words used are often related to qualities or traits that need to be emphasized (or even overcome) in the individual. Foreign words or phrases can be associated with a past-life experience.

Wreath

Associated with that which encircles or surrounds. A Christmas wreath might indicate the Christ spirit.

Yin/Yang

Can correspond to balance. Associated with the male/female energies.

Zodiac: Aquarius ≈

Positively associated with idealism and humanitarianism. Negatively associated with unpredictability and being opinionated. Might indicate one who is prone to eccentricity.

Zodiac: Aries ♈

Positively associated with leadership abilities, being direct, energetic, and courageous. Negatively associated with self-ishness, impulsiveness, and having a quick temper.

Zodiac: Cancer ♋   Positively associated with a love for the home and sensitivity. Negatively associated with being overly emotional and being prone to self-pity. Might indicate one who is prone to jealousy.

Zodiac: Capricorn ♑   Positively associated with reliability, patience and humor. Negatively associated with being overly rigid, cheap, and prone to being discontented or pessimistic.

Zodiac: Gemini ♊   Positively associated with communication, the mind, versatility, and intelligence. Negatively associated with restlessness, inconsistency, and being prone to gossip.

Zodiac: Leo ♌   Positively associated with broadmindedness, organizational skills, and being generous. Negatively associated with aggressiveness, intolerance, and being opinionated. Might correspond to one who is prone to being willful and headstrong.

Zodiac: Libra ♎   Positively associated with balance, idealism, fairness, and diplomacy. Negatively associated with indecisiveness and being easily influenced by others.

Zodiac: Pisces ♓   Positively associated with humility, spirituality, and intuition. Negatively associated with being impractical, vague, and overly secretive or anxious. Might correspond to a commitment to spiritual truths.

Zodiac: Sagittarius ♐   Positively associated with optimism, adaptability, and sincerity. Negatively associated with restlessness, carelessness, and being prone to exaggeration. Might indicate one who is prone to extremes or self-interest. Could indicate one who loves freedom and exploring.

Zodiac: **Scorpio** ♏   Positively associated with persistence, determination, and discernment. Negatively associated with jealousy, introversion, callousness, and being prone to sexual excess. Might correspond to a sense of purposefulness.

Zodiac: **Taurus** ♉   Positively associated with dependability, practicality, stability, and endurance. Negatively associated with stubbornness, possessiveness, and being obsessive.

Zodiac: **Virgo** ♍   Positively associated with modesty, an analytical mind, and being neat and tidy. Negatively associated with worry, being too conventional, and prone to criticism.

Appendix B:
Edgar Cayce's Symbolism
for the Revelation

666—Mark of the Beast	Any group, organization, or affiliation that believes it can exist apart from the influence of God. Associated with the lower nature of humankind that places its faith in man-made activities alone. Also corresponds with supplanting the will of God in preference to personal will.
144,000	The perfectly functioning cells that have been "sealed" within the physical body and are waiting to be awakened in order to influence and harmonize all other cells.

	Associated with 12,000 spiritualized cells within each of the twelve major systems/structures of the body. See Twelve Tribes.
Anti-Christ	Internal motivations in opposition to the spirit of love, joy, obedience, long-suffering, kindness, and brotherly love. That which is in opposition to the spirit of the Christ. Associated with hate, contention, strife, faultfinding, and selfishness.
Armageddon	Associated with the conflict within self between the spiritual nature of the soul and the material/physical urges and desires that have been acquired by the individual in the earth.
Army of Two Hundred Thousand Thousand Horsemen	Corresponds to the sounding of the sixth trumpet and the second woe. These are symbolic of the multitude of destructive forces within the individual that continue to be incompatible with the attunement process.
Babylon	Symbolic of the lower self.
Beast, Coming up out of the Earth	Corresponds to the gonad center and the individual's motivation of self-sustenance feeling threatened by the establishment of a higher spiritual ideal. See False Prophet.
Beast, Rising out of the Sea	Associated with the cells of Leydig and the individual's motivation of self-propagation rising up in rebellion.
Black Horse	Associated with the opening of the second seal and the messenger hormones of the cells of Leydig.

Book of Life	Symbolic of the Akashic Records or the soul memory of the individual.
Bride	Symbolic of the purified higher self.
Calf (or Ox)	Corresponds to the first spiritual center and the gonads. See Church of Ephesus and Four Beasts.
Child, Travailing in Birth	Corresponds to the birth of the universal Christ ideal within the individual. See Universal Christ Consciousness.
Church of Ephesus	First spiritual center, associated with the gonads. Corresponds to the opening of the first seal and the vision of the white horse. The virtue is patience. The fault is falling away from the love of God. Also associated with the figure of the calf.
Church of Laodicea	Seventh spiritual center, associated with the pituitary. Corresponds to the opening of the seventh seal and the vision of silence. The fault/virtue is being neither hot nor cold.
Church of Pergamos	Third spiritual center, associated with the adrenals (solar plexus). Corresponds to the opening of the third seal and the vision of the red horse. The virtue is faithfulness. The fault is casting stumbling blocks before others. Also associated with the figure of the lion.
Church of Philadelphia	Sixth spiritual center, associated with the pineal. Corresponds to the opening of the sixth seal and the vision of the earthquake. The virtue is an open door. There is no fault.

Church of Sardis

Fifth spiritual center, associated with the thyroid. Corresponds to the opening of the fifth seal and the vision of the souls of the perfect slain. The virtue is few not defiled. The fault is imperfect works.

Church of Smyrna

Second spiritual center, associated with the cells of Leydig (lyden). Corresponds to the opening of the second seal and the vision of the black horse. The virtue is dealing with tribulation (suffering). The fault is insincerity. Also associated with the figure of the man.

Church of Thyatira

Fourth spiritual center, associated with the thymus. Corresponds to the opening of the fourth seal and the vision of the pale horse. The virtue is charity (love) and service. The fault is fornication. Also associated with the figure of the eagle.

Eagle

Corresponds to the fourth spiritual center and the thymus. See Church of Thyatira and Four Beasts.

Earth

Representative of the physical body or the individual's material self. See Four Elements.

Earthquake

Associated with the opening of the sixth seal and the messenger hormones of the pineal.

Egypt

Associated with the bondage of self.

Eye

Symbolic of the activity of awareness.

False Prophet

Corresponds to an immature level of spiritual development. Associated with a stage at which an individual may be able

	to manifest spiritual gifts, such as healing and psychic ability (even miracles), but has not completed the revelation of self. Identified with the Beast Coming up out of the Earth.
Fire	Can be symbolic of the process of purification and purging. See Four Elements.
Flood Coming out of the Serpent's Mouth	Symbolic of the flood of emotions within self that can rise up in fear and rebellion.
Four Angels at the Four Corners of the Earth	Associated with the four forces or influences that affect humankind: environment, heredity, mental influences (also associated with planes of consciousness), and spiritual influences (also corresponding to the influence of previous lives).
Four Beasts	Represents the four lower centers/motivational influences within each individual and symbolized by the calf, man, lion, and eagle. Associated with the motivations of self-gratification (thymus = eagle), self-preservation (adrenals = lion), self-propagation (cells of Leydig = man), and self-sustenance (gonads = calf).
Four Elements (Air, Water, Fire, and Earth)	The four elements correspond to the four lower spiritual centers, as follows: air = thymus; fire = adrenals; water = cells of Leydig; and, earth = gonads.
Frogs	Representative of the uncleanness or that which is out of attunement that must be overcome in self.
Golden Censer	Represents the acts of goodness that rise (much like incense rises) before the throne of God.

Golden Reed	Corresponds to the measurement of divine understanding and a divine purpose that has been attained.
Great Multitude	Corresponds to all of the cells of the human body.
Hidden Manna	Associated with the spiritual sustenance and understanding that becomes available to any that remained steadfast in faith.
Horn	Symbolic of the activity of desire.
In the Spirit	Corresponds to being in a state of meditation and communion with the divine.
Lake of Fire	A perpetual state of purification under the control of the higher self or the divine.
Lamb	Associated with the universal Christ Consciousness or the universal Christ ideal. See Universal Christ Consciousness. May also be associated with a gentle, obedient spirit.
Lion	Corresponds to the third spiritual center and the adrenals. See Church of Pergamos and Four Beasts.
Little Book that is Sweet in the Mouth and Bitter in the Belly	Associated with the knowledge that relates to the threefold nature of the self in terms of the physical, the mental, and the spiritual forces. It is sweet in the mouth because it is wonderful to attain. It is bitter in the belly because it must be personally applied repeatedly (in many experiences, before many people, even in many lifetimes).

Locusts	Associated with the sounding of the fifth trumpet and the first woe. These are symbolic of the lower bodily forces, vibrations, and influences that remain out of harmony with the Whole.
Man	Corresponds to the second spiritual center and the cells of Leydig. See Church of Smyrna and Four Beasts.
Michael, the Archangel	Associated with those spiritual forces that would assist, guide, and protect the individual on his or her path toward enlightenment. Cayce called Michael, "the Lord of the Way."
Morning Star	Associated with the planet Venus, which is the planet symbolic of love. Corresponds to the divine love that becomes a part of the individual who cultivates the virtue of the fourth center. See Church of Thyatira.
Multitude that Stood Before the Throne	Represents the rest of the body in the process of spiritualization.
Names not Written in the Book of Life	Symbolic of the rebellious aspects within self that cannot be in keeping with the oneness of the divine. Also associated with the imperfected cellular structures that are out of attunement with the Whole.
New Jerusalem	Symbolizes the dominion of the higher self. Corresponds to the holy city and therefore the soul's higher purposes and experiences.
New Name	Symbolic of achieving the selfhood and fulfilling the specific purpose intended for each and every individual. Also cor-

	responds to the unique and individual name assigned by the Creator for each individual. See White Stone.
Pale Horse	Associated with the opening of the fourth seal and the messenger hormones of the thymus.
Red Dragon, having Seven Heads and Ten Horns	Symbolic of the rebellious forces within self that would attempt to destroy a higher spiritual ideal.
Red Horse	Associated with the opening of the third seal and the messenger hormones of the adrenals.
Reed Like Unto a Rod (to Measure the Temple)	This corresponds to the activity of deciding how all encompassing each individual's understanding of the love of God and the brother-sisterhood of humankind is going to be. In other words, will it be limited to one denomination or will it include everyone?
Sea of Glass	Can correspond to the stilled emotions during the process of meditation. Might also correlate to the stilled energy of the kundalini.
Second Death	Symbolic of becoming subservient to the desires and fears of the lower self in spite of having obtained for a time a higher level of understanding and awareness.
Seven Angels with Seven Vials	Represents meeting the karmic memory of self at the level of each of the seven spiritual centers. The soul memory receptacles that correspond to each of the seven centers are symbolized by the seven vials. The seven angels are the points of

contact between the spiritual and the physical at each of these seven centers.

Seven Churches

The seven spiritual centers/chakras (associated with the endocrine glands) within the physical body. Associated with the gonads (first church, Ephesus), cells of Leydig (second church, Smyrna), adrenals (third church, Pergamos), thymus (fourth church, Thyatira), thyroid (fifth church, Sardis), pineal (sixth church, Philadelphia), and the pituitary (seventh church, Laodicea). See individual churches.

Seven Golden Candlesticks

Corresponds to the seven endocrine centers within the physical body as well as the seven churches and the seven spiritual centers/chakras. See Seven Churches.

Seven Mountains (or Seven Heads of the Beast)

The seven mountains or seven heads of the beast that the whore of Babylon sits upon represent her seat of power and dominion over each of the seven centers of the body. The imagery symbolizes that the desires of the lower self have become the ruling force in the individual.

Seven Plagues

Indicates the purification, conquering, and cleansing of "errors" that have been a part of the soul's history. Can be associated with each of the seven spiritual centers/chakras. See Seven Churches.

Seven Spirits Before the Throne

The seven spirits that are before the throne are symbolic of the points of contact between the spiritual chakras and the physical body. See Seven Churches.

Seven Stars	Aspects of the divine spirit associated with each of the seven spiritual centers chakras. Can correspond to each of the seven dimensions/planetary realms. See Seven Churches.
Seven Trumpets Sounded by Seven Angels	Corresponds to the process of physical purification, especially as it relates to each of the seven spiritual centers. See Seven Churches.
Seven-Sealed Book	The human body with its seven spiritual centers. See Seven Churches.
Silence in Heaven	Associated with the opening of the seventh seal and the messenger hormones of the pituitary. Imagery is also suggestive of the practice of meditation.
Sodom	Can correspond to sin/error as well as selfishness.
Souls of Faithful Slain	Associated with the opening of the fifth seal and the messenger hormones of the thyroid.
Sung a New Song	Symbolic of the new experience of being in accord with the spirit that is made available to each individual that reaches this level of attunement.
Temple of God is Opened	Indicates that the self may become attuned to the superconsciousness of the divine. Corresponds to entering into the most holy place of the temple of self.
Temple of the Tabernacle of the Testimony in Heaven being Opened	Associated with the opening of the Book of Life or the Akashic Records. Symbolic of the soul memories of the individual being revealed.

Ten Horns (or Ten Kings)	Associated with the conflicting urges (desires) within each of the five senses that war with one another.
Ten Thousand Times Ten Thousand, and Thousands of Thousands	Corresponds to all of the cells of the human body.
Thousand Years	The imagery of the dragon being bound in the bottomless pit for a thousand years is suggestive of the rebellious spirit being contained for a time within the confines of the lower self. It also suggests the fact that for a thousand years only those souls who have chosen a higher spiritual ideal will be allowed to incarnate in the earth.
Twelve Gates (Twelve Foundations)	Symbolic of the twelve purified structures of the body or the purified pathways of the twelve pairs of cranial nerves.
Twelve Pearls (Twelve Gates)	Associated with wisdom and enlightenment.
Twelve Precious Stones	Represents the perfection and great worth that has been achieved through hardship.
Twelve Tribes	Associated with the twelve major structures/systems of the body, as follows: Osteology (the bones); Joints and Ligaments; Muscles and Fasciae (connective tissue); Circulatory System (heart, arteries, and veins); Lymphatic System; Nervous System (central and peripheral); Organs of the Senses; Integument (the skin); Respiratory System; Digestive System; Urogenital System (urinary and reproductive organs); and, Endocrine Glands.

Twenty-Four Elders	The twenty-four cranial nerves (twelve pair) within the head, especially as they relate to the five senses: sight, hearing, taste, smell, and touch.
Two Candlesticks	Associated with the Two Witnesses. See Two Witnesses.
Two Olive Trees	Associated with the Two Witnesses. See Two Witnesses.
Two Wings of a Great Eagle	Corresponds with rising above the material and mental and transitioning instead to things of a spiritual nature.
Two Witnesses	Corresponds to two of the four influences that affect humankind: mental urges, associated with various planes of consciousness; and, spiritual influences, due to previous incarnations. Also associated with the subconscious and superconscious aspects of an individual. Symbolized by the two olive trees as well as the two candlesticks.
Universal Christ Consciousness (Ultimate or Universal Ideal)	The awareness within each soul, imprinted in pattern on the mind and waiting to be awakened by the will, of the soul's oneness with God.
War in Heaven	Conflict between one's spiritual ideal and material and selfish concerns.
White Horse	Associated with the opening of the first seal and the messenger hormones of the gonads.
White Horse upon which Sits one called Faithful and True.	Symbolic of the messenger of attunement and the spirit of the universal Christ ideal that influences the entire body. See Universal Christ Consciousness.

White Stone

Corresponds to the purity that results for all those who undergo hardship, endure, and fulfill their mission in life. See New Name.

Whore of Babylon

Symbolic of the lower self. Representative of how the soul in its passage through time and space has become overwhelmed ("drunken") by its own desires, power, and selfishness.

Winepress of the Wrath of God

The additional work and refinement required in order to become purified before the throne of God.

Woman Clothed with the Sun

Represents all of those experiences in the earth and materiality that have brought the individual to this point in time.

Appendix C:
References and Recommended Reading

A.R.E. Meditation Course. A.R.E. Press: Virginia Beach, Virginia. 1978.

Argüelles, José. *The Transformative Vision.* Berkeley, California: Shambala Publications, Inc. 1975.

Barker, William P. *Everyone in the Bible.* Fleming H. Revell Company: Westwood, New Jersey. 1966.

Cayce, Edgar. *A Commentary on the Book of Revelation.* A.R.E. Press: Virginia Beach, Virginia. 1995.

Cayce, Edgar. *Auras: An Essay on the Meaning of Colors.* A.R.E. Press: Virginia Beach, Virginia. 1973.

Cayce, Edgar (readings). Edgar Cayce Foundation: Virginia Beach, Virginia. 1971, 1993-2007.

Cayce, Hugh Lynn. *Faces of Fear: Overcoming Life's Anxieties.* Harper & Row: San Francisco. 1980.

Cayce, Hugh Lynn. "Snow White and the Seven Dwarfs," public lecture. Virginia Beach, Virginia. August 1969.

Cerminara, Gina. "Archetypes and Aura Charts." *Bulletin.* Association for Research and Enlightenment, Inc.: Virginia Beach, Virginia. 1946.

The Edgar Cayce Dream Dictionary. A.R.E. Press: Virginia Beach, Virginia. 1986.

Gibran, Kahlil. *The Prophet.* Alfred A. Knopf: New York. 1987.

Gray, Henry. *Anatomy of the Human Body.* Lea & Febiger: Philadelphia. 1973.

Hamilton, Edith and Huntington Cairns, editors. *Plato: The Collected Dialogues.* Bollingen Series, Princeton University Press: Princeton, New Jersey. 1961.

The Holy Bible. King James Version.

Irion, J. Everett. *Interpreting the Revelation with Edgar Cayce.* A.R.E. Press: Virginia Beach, Virginia. 1982.

The Jewish Encyclopedia. Funk and Wagnalls: London. 1901.

Jung, C.G. *Memories, Dreams, Reflections.* Vintage Books: New York. 1989.

Jung, C.G. *Mandala Symbolism.* Bollingen Series, Princeton University Press: Princeton, New Jersey. 1973.

Jung, C.G. *Collected Works, Volume 14.* Bollingen Series, Princeton University Press: Princeton, New Jersey. 1967.

Jung, C.G., editor. *Man and His Symbols.* Dell Publishing: New York. 1968.

Lane, Barbara, Ph.D. *Sixteen Clues to Your Past Lives: A Guide to Discovering Who You Were.* A.R.E. Press: Virginia Beach, Virginia. 1999.

Manheim, Ralph, translator. *Grimms' Tales for Young and Old.* Anchor Books: New York. 1983.

McGarey, Gladys, T., M.D., M.D. (H). *Dopey's Path to Enlightenment.* Inkwell Productions: Scottsdale, Arizona. 2002.

Puryear, Herbert B., Ph.D. "The Revelation: Keys to Christian Mysticism," public lecture. Virginia Beach, Virginia. June 1983.

Puryear, Herbert B., Ph.D. *Why Jesus Taught Reincarnation.* New Paradigm Press: Scottsdale, Arizona. 1992.

Puryear, Herbert B., Ph.D. *Covenant* "Lessons XXII & XXIII——Study Self! Study the Revelation!" Association for Research and Enlightenment, Inc.: Virginia Beach, Virginia. 1979.

Shelley, Violet. *Symbols and the Self.* A.R.E. Press: Virginia Beach, Virginia. 1986.

Swann, Ingo. "History of the Edgar Cayce Aurachart [painting]." Edgar Cayce Foundation archives: Virginia Beach, Virginia. 1971.

Todeschi, Kevin J. *Edgar Cayce on the Akashic Records.* A.R.E. Press: Virginia Beach, Virginia. 1999.

Todeschi, Kevin J. *Dream Images and Symbols.* A.R.E. Press: Virginia Beach, Virginia. 2004..

Van Auken, John. *Edgar Cayce on the Revelation.* A.R.E. Press: Virginia Beach, Virginia. 2000.

Walters, Derek. *Chinese Mythology.* Aquarian Press: London. 1992.

Werner, E.T.C. *Myths and Legends of China.* George G. Harrap & Co.: London. 1922.